Faith
Through
Trial

Faith Through Trial

A true story of hope and survival

By
Dr. Thanh Van Anderson
Bruce M. Baker

Soonershoot Press
Oklahoma City, Oklahoma

ISBN: 978-1-7361995-5-8

Library of Congress Control Number: 2022903082

Cover photo:
Photo **111214541** © **Vinh Dao** | **Dreamstime.com**

All events portrayed in this book are true.
Details expressed are a combination of memory and gleanings from historical writing from and about the period.

Contents

Dedication

I want to dedicate this book to all cancer patients, especially those I met at the Tucson Oncology Cancer Center during my ten years as a volunteer. I met so many wonderful people, many of whom are still my friends. I was blessed to be a part of their lives. I believe now as I did then. God allowed me to have liver cancer to experience life through the lens of cancer patients, which, although different from their journey, gave me some understanding of what they had to go through.

Having cancer is not always a death sentence. More and more people survive this cursed disease every day, but the journey is tough. We often feel we fight this battle alone because our family members and friends have no idea what a cancer patient must go through. Nevertheless, I always felt one person was there for me all the time – Jesus Christ.

During my illness, I felt closer to God, actually felt his presence within me. That was a turning point for me. I had always considered myself a Christian from my youth and felt strong in my faith. Cancer took me to the next level. I never had a close relationship with Jesus until I had cancer. I talked to God often and decided to turn my cancer completely over to him. God held my life in his hands. I understood that my worrying would not change anything.

I also would like to dedicate this book to my Father, Nguyen Giao Huan, and Shady K. Anderson, my late husband. My father was my first teacher, who had taught me the meaning of honesty, hard work, fairness, dignity, Christianity, and loyalty — the foundation of an individual's character. My husband was my rock. He always supported me in every aspect of my life. He was always there to help me spiritually, emotionally, and physically.

I would also like to thank my sisters Vinh, Tracy, and Phan, my brother, He, my sister-in-law Anna, my daughter Helena, and my brother-in-law Robert for never failing to make time to be with me, to take care of me. Since my pancreatic cancer diagnosis in July 2019, my family members have been taking turns coming to Tucson to take care of me during the chemo treatments and my pancreas cancer surgery. Since their retirement, my brother, Nguyen Gia He, and my sister-in-law Anna Nguyen have also come to Tucson to take care of me.

I like to thank Pastor Peter and Sister Sheila Kraft and other members of Eastside Assembly of God in Tucson, the churches in Vietnam for faithfully praying for me all these years, and for the many friends in Tucson, Oklahoma, and other States for their continuous support and prayer. I would also like to thank Dr. Martine Beachboard for the many hours she has spent helping me with this book. She has spent so much time, and her assistance was invaluable. I would also like to thank Dr. Paul Nakazato, Dr. Carlos Boras, Dr. James Michael Darragh, Dr. Taylor S. Riall and Dr. Rachna Shroff for their expertise, caring and the many hours they have given me beyond their duties.

A special thanks to Mr. Bruce M Baker for his willingness to take my thoughts and put them on paper. I was so touched when I talked to him, and he accepted the assignment. He is a great writer. I read the "The Chance" that he wrote with Lisa Cheng, and I couldn't put it down. The story was great, and Mr. Baker did an amazing job making the story so interesting. I also want to thank Lisa Cheng for her support. I have known Lisa for a long time but had never heard the story of her struggle. Lisa, you are an amazing young lady!

Many successes have blessed me during my life, but I have faced many trials also – the latest being my current journey with pancreatic cancer. Of my victories, I am most proud of my educational journey, from "Me know English" to receiving my doctorate in Education and, finally, becoming the first Vietnamese to hold a senior position with the Oklahoma State Department of Education, Director of Bilingual Education.

I welcome you to join my journey and witness the hands of God guiding me through my last minutes in this world. I am going through trials, but I also have peace, for Jesus is always with me, as He has said.

"I have told you these things so that in me you may have peace. In this world, you will have trouble, but take heart! I have overcome the world" John 16:33

I know God can heal us, but sometimes God allows us to go through these difficult trials for a reason. We will always have problems in our lives, but those problems come differently for each person. Please don't give up; cancer might have our bodies but not our souls.

Thanh Van Anderson

My First Life - Vietnam

Chapter 1

"Blessed is the man who trusts in the LORD And whose trust is the LORD. 8 "For he will be like a tree planted by the water, That extends its roots by a stream And will not fear when the heat comes; But its leaves will be green, And it will not be anxious in a year of drought Nor cease to yield fruit."

(Jeremiah 17:7-8).

I am no stranger to Death. Death and I are old friends and have met on several occasions. My God reminded me that there was more to do each time and told Death to wait. God cured me of liver cancer and hepatitis-C. To be sure, medical science played its part, but I believe that faith brought me back to health. Now, I feel that my reprieve is over. Barring another divine intervention, I feel certain that I will take Death's hand as old friends and go to my new home this time.

I clearly remember the first time my doctor told me I had liver cancer. My life slammed to a screeching stop. I saw the doctor's mouth moving, but the words didn't make any sense to me. I felt my knees sag as though they were incapable of supporting me anymore. I asked my God how this could happen. After all, I was a good church-going woman. I had lived a good life. Why would this happen to me? My world was crumbling around me.

At first, I didn't want anyone but my husband to know. I did not want to bother family and friends with what I considered a "personal problem." I was wrong. I told my sister, Phan, first. I couldn't believe how much better I felt after letting her share my burden.

Later, I called to tell my friends, looking for sympathy and caring words. Some responded with love. I could feel it soaring over the phone lines. They called me every day, asking how I was and if I needed anything. They helped me to find my life again. Other friends said how sorry they were and how unfair it was and never called again. It was as if they couldn't handle the presence of cancer in their lives. They needed to cut it out – remove its presence – remove me. I found myself angry with them for their rejection.

I questioned God about my disease and, through my faith, found healing love in His presence. He calmed me from within and allowed me to look at my situation. With time, I realized that my life was not over just because I had this disease. Every day was a gift to cherish and hold in my heart.

I remembered that people died every day from many causes, many of them sudden – in the blink of the proverbial eye. Finally, my most important lesson was realizing that I could only deal with things that I controlled. I had no control over this cancer growing inside of me. That responsibility fell to my medical team and my God.

From my first bout of cancer, I could hear God telling me to write my story down on paper and tell others about my trials and victories. I asked him, "How should I do this?" English is my third language. I could speak and write Vietnamese, but that was not the audience for this writing. I had French in primary school, but what little expertise I had at the time was now long gone. He responded to me with a scripture passage that I read that evening. *Return to your home and declare how much God has done for you."* (Luke 8:39). I realized then that God would provide a way to make my record known.

The tale I wish to share is a story of faith and life, and like any good narrative, I must start at the beginning. My story begins in 1950 over eight thousand miles from here in the tiny village of Tu Chau just south of Hanoi, Vietnam, the place where I was born.

My parents, along with the people of Tu Chau, were rice growers as the town lay in the flood plain of the Red River, making rice easier to grow. We were people of faith as well as of the soil. The French missionaries had brought Catholicism to our village many years ago, and we followed the priests' teachings with enthusiasm.

Although Mother was very knowledgeable about farming – father was not. Her parents had left her a great deal of farmland while his parents had given him a fine brick house. Since he was more educated and not proficient at farming, he became one of the local schoolteachers and the choir director at the Catholic Church. She managed the farms and the workers who cared for them. We had a good life.

Tu Chau was also my first introduction to death.

Death had surrounded my village for decades. First, my ancestors had fought the Chinese, then, more recently, the French, and when those battles weren't enough – we fought with each other. The deaths from those wars haunted the stories my father told me while growing up.

It wasn't until I was three years old, the youngest of three girls, that death became intimate with me. My beloved mother died while giving birth to my little brother, who also died.

Even though I was very young, I remember her funeral vividly. The three of us all wore white clothing as the villagers carried her coffin into the house. I tried to get Mother's attention, but she acted as though she couldn't see me. The three of us walked around the coffin again and again until finally, tired and sleepy, I just wanted to go to bed, and I wanted my mother to take me there.

I called and cried for her at the top of my lungs. None of the hugs from family or friends would satisfy me. I wanted my mother; only she would do. At long last, exhaustion took its toll. I fell asleep on the floor beside the coffin with my mother lying silently inside. I never saw her again.

For many years, until I was old enough to understand, Father would tell me stories about where she was. She had "gone to buy salt" or "was visiting friends." Eventually, enough time passed, and I just stopped asking him, but her image never faded from my heart.

Not long after Mother's death, Father rented our land to the workers and took a job in Hanoi. After that, we only saw him on the weekend. My sister, Luyen, only twelve years old, took responsibility for Phan, age seven, and myself, a mere four. Often, we would wander over to our aunts and uncles, begging for food. They fed us when they could, but I can't remember anyone ever reaching out to help us.

Father always gave Luyen money before he left for Hanoi; he just didn't teach her how to budget or, better yet, teach her to trade rice for other things we needed. She would overspend on some things and then not have enough left for food. Luyen didn't even know how to cook. Her rice was either underdone or burned.

In Vietnam, there is a saying, "Mo coi cha an com voi ca, mo coi me liem la ngoai cho." Roughly translated, it means, if your dad dies, you will eat rice with fish, but if your mother dies, you will be so poor that there would be nothing to eat, and you will have to lick the leaf wrappers. It was almost that bad.

Don't misunderstand me. Our father did care for us. He would return from Hanoi every Saturday night with money, food, and candies. Father would pull me aside and tell me that Mother had sent them just for me because I was such a good girl. I was happy to get the candy but would have much rather had the sweet smell of my mother's skin. We didn't have too long to worry about it. Once again, our world was about to change. His stay in Hanoi lasted less than a year.

In May of 1954, the forces of Ho Chi Minh dealt a fatal blow to the French at the battle of Dien Bien Phu, effectively ending six years of warfare against the Europeans. Later, in July of that same year, the French and the new Democratic Republic of Vietnam signed an accord in Geneva, Switzerland – a half a world away.

That agreement effectively split the country in two. The North would be under socialist rule led by Ho Chi Minh. The South would be under self-rule under the figurehead of the former Vietnamese emperor, Bao Dai, and an elected president.

Anyone on either side of the 17th parallel – the demarcation line separating the two entities who wanted to go to the other side, had three hundred days to do so before the respective governments sealed the border. Both sides agreed to transport any civilians desiring to move. Rumors were that the Communist North threatened to ban our Catholic faith, so my father elected to move south along with many villagers in our community.

After that, things moved very quickly. We had only three days to make the necessary arrangements to sell or distribute our property. My dad sold some rice fields and furniture but gave most of the lands and belongings, along with his house, to my Uncle Ket. He was one of three uncles who had decided to stay in North Vietnam. It wasn't that he didn't want to go; it was just that his wife was too sick to travel.

Even though I was still very young, I clearly remember watching our village fade in the distance as we walked away, leaving our uncle and other friends and neighbors behind. There was a long walk ahead of us. The transport trucks would not come into our village; the official departure point was in another town – Ha Tri, about twenty kilometers away.

I remember a lot of tears as we left. I was very young at the time, so I didn't have many friends. My sisters, on the other hand, did. They seemed to be attached to every boy and girl in the village. They cried so much during our goodbyes that I cried out of sympathy for their loss.

Of course, not everyone stayed behind. Many, if not most, were traveling with us – especially the members of our Catholic community. The Catholic priest had been preaching about the Communist ways, that Communists were atheists and did not believe in God. In China and other Communist lands, the government denied Christians the right to worship. He had no doubt but that the same things would happen here. He also played an important part in arranging our relocation with the authorities.

Some of the other priests remained in the North with those parishioners that either would not or could not migrate south. They wanted to do all they could to provide spiritual support and guidance for those left behind. Many of the other priests came with us. They reminded us that our community had once built a church and school in Tu Chau. We would construct another at our destination in the south. Our community would continue.

Each refugee was limited to only one bag. My dad and my two sisters stuffed cookware and their clothing into their large bags. Slowly, hindered by the weight of our belongings, we made our way to Ha Tri together. Being with others made the miles not so long.

Once we arrived, we stayed in an old warehouse building for a few days. People from all over the region gathered here. So many people wanted to leave that there were not enough government vehicles to take us from Ha Tri to Hanoi all at once. We had to take turns.

After several days, our turn finally came. We loaded into the military vehicles and went to Hanoi. Once there, we waited for another day before flying to the South. I don't remember much about the flight. The French and American militaries and some private air carriers had agreed to fly us to Saigon in South Vietnam. I was just glad we didn't have to walk.

The journey was hard for us, but it seemed especially so for my dad. Not only had he left all his material possessions, his house, and his land behind, he had also left my mother buried in the northern soil. Now, he found himself in a new land with new customs. Even though he was still in Vietnam, the differences between the north and the south were large. He knew very well that he was not only responsible for his life, but he also had sole responsibility for the three of us – the oldest being a child of twelve. The weight must have been incredible.

The South Vietnamese authorities tried to keep our village together for the most part. First, they sent us to a series of temporary relocation areas, basically army camps, where we were housed in small tents and fed in a mess hall.

We stayed there until the authorities found a permanent location for us. The town was Cu Chi, a district of Binh Duong Province, located just fifty kilometers northwest of Saigon. There were no houses in the part of the village where we went. Those we would need to build ourselves.

Building a house was not that unusual. We often built mud houses in the north, so the villagers thought it was perfectly normal here. People from the village and a few paid builders worked together to build mud houses for the families. The mud homes started with a framework of tree trunks that supported the structure. Then, the builders used mud, tree branches, and grasses to form a kind of thatch that made up the walls and roof. The sun's intense heat did the rest. After it was dry, a lime wash and some cement gave the walls a smooth finish.

Phan and I were too small to help, but I believe that Luyen worked on the house alongside my father. I never knew how the villagers decided who would live where, but, in the end, my family ended up sharing a duplex with the family of Mr. Su. The entire house only had two rooms. We lived in the room on the right side, and Mr. Su's family lived in the room on the left.

Cu Chi was a drier area than the Red River valley in the north. Rice wouldn't grow here, and, unfortunately, that was all the people knew how to grow. So, we changed.

Instead of rice, we grew vegetables and peanuts, crops more suitable for the soil. Some people changed even further. They decided to manufacture fireworks. Our village soon became famous throughout the country for the quality of the fireworks we made. They had named their brand Tu Chau after our old village in the North, and the fireworks business prospered.

Making fireworks was dangerous – deadly so. My father didn't want to risk leaving his daughters orphaned. Orphans didn't fare any better here than they had in the North. Instead, he got a position as a teacher at a public elementary school. My sisters went to his school; however, since I was still too young for public school, my father enrolled me at the Catholic school a mile from my home. I would have to walk to and from there every day.

The weather was very hot and humid in this part of Vietnam, much warmer than at Tu Chau. In South Vietnam, we only had two seasons – wet and dry. We had no need for spring, summer, fall and winter. The temperature varied little from one month to the next. More than once, I begged God to send a cloud to block the sun from shining directly on me. As if the oppressive weather wasn't enough, dogs often chased after me as I walked down the street.

Many people in Cu Chi owned dogs, and I believed that most lived on my way to school. The problem was that there was no place for them to go except to run on the streets. No one had a fence or anything like that.

I remember one time when several dogs chased

me down the street. I was so scared. I had nowhere to go. I don't believe that I have ever prayed so hard for a miracle – for God to save me from their feral jaws. Suddenly, for no apparent reason, all the dogs stopped chasing me simultaneously. The timing was not coincidental. I firmly believed that God had heard my prayer. I never doubted that God was always there for me from this point forward.

If the weather and the dogs weren't enough, I also got harassed by my cousin, Hue, who was a few years older than me. Despite the age difference, she was in the same class as me. Many times, Hue didn't do her homework, and she would force me to give her all the answers. She threatened to beat me up if I didn't do it. Even if I did, she would still pull my ears or punch me.

The persecution finally got to the point that I told my dad, and he talked to her mother. After that, she never bothered me again. Even as a young child, I was very close to God and spoke to Him often. I always believed that God would hear me when I prayed and that his grace would bless me.

I was old enough to go to public school with my father and sisters the next year. This change made me very happy until I discovered that my first-grade teacher was my dad. Even then, I realized that having your father as your teacher was a mixed blessing.

On the one hand, I could always ask him questions at home about things at school. On the other hand, I tended to get harsher punishments for infractions at school. Truthfully, I was positive that I got more spankings than the other students. I remember one time when I accidentally fell asleep in class. My dad rubbed chalk on my face. When that didn't wake me, the laughter of my friends did. I was so embarrassed! I never slept in his or any other class again.

Despite the consequences I had to face, I was no angel. I tried everything, and sometimes 'everything' involved bending or even breaking a few rules. When caught, I always admitted my error and paid the consequences for my actions.

Every morning, I would get up and go to church and then ride to school with my dad on our bicycles. Sometimes, I was too sleepy to ride carefully and fell, but dad didn't see me. I called after him, but it didn't help. Dad rode so fast that he didn't hear me fall, and soon he was gone. I would have to pick myself up and hurry off to school, praying that I wouldn't be late. Tardiness meant a spanking by the school principal, and I didn't want that to happen again.

All in all, those first years in the south were mostly pleasant. Gradually, we adapted to our new country and its customs and practices. Slowly, our connections with those we had left behind grew distant. There wasn't much communication between the south and north during this time. Our roots dug deeper into the southern soil that we now called home slowly, yet surely.

Chapter 2

"There is an appointed time for everything. And there is a time for every event under heaven."
(Ecclesiastes 3:1)

Even with the trials of moving and adjusting to life in the South, the four of us seemed quite happy with our new circumstances. As my sisters and I grew older, we found friends among our fellow villagers. Lost in our girlish thoughts, we never considered how Father might feel. We never fully understood the problems of taking care of three girls. We never entertained the possibility that he needed someone else to share his life.

Now, my father was still a good-looking man, so we shouldn't have been surprised when the lady who owned the tailor shop turned out to like my dad – a lot. Americans might think it strange that my father would go to a tailor, let alone go often, but we do things differently in Vietnam. If we needed new clothes, we would purchase material and take it to the tailor shop to have the clothing handmade.

Father seemed to be taken with her as well. However, she was from the South and was not Catholic, and for my father, that would not do. Additionally, my dad didn't know that much about her. He worried about what kind of stepmother she would be to his girls. In the end, he decided not to pursue the relationship.

Not long after he had abandoned his association with the tailor, a lady moved to our village from Ho Nai who loved to play matchmaker. We called her Aunty Khuyen. When she heard that my dad was thinking of marrying again, she talked to him about a young woman from her old village. That woman later became my stepmother, **Hoang thi Noi.**

According to Aunty Khuyen, she was a very sweet, kind, caring person. She was also an orphan. She lost her mother when she was quite young and then watched as the Communists executed her father with her stepmother at her side.

She and her stepmother fled to the south a few years later. Even though she was fifteen years younger than my father, she had experienced more than her years should have allowed.

My father requested an introduction where he could meet Noi. The meeting was to take place in her village, about six hours away from ours. When dad made the trip to see her, I got to come with him and my Uncle Chung while my sisters had to stay at home taking care of the house.

During the gathering, I sat beside my dad taking in all that was happening. Then I saw her, Noi, for the first time as she served us food. She was very pretty. My father thought so as well. Even though the party was to introduce them to each other, I don't believe the two of them had any time alone the entire evening. In the end, my dad based his decision completely on her looks and what people told him about her.

The wedding lasted for two days partly because Cu Chi was so far away from Ho Nai by car. Our father arranged for some of our relatives to come early to help prepare food for the wedding. Once again, my sisters had to stay home for some reason while I got to accompany my father to Ho Nai.

The wedding took place in the village church. My aunts and I got to sit in the front pew where I could see everything happening. It was all very exciting. I remember thinking how handsome my father was in his black suit and how beautiful his bride dressed in her white ao dai, a traditional Vietnamese dress, with her long black hair hanging down to her knees. I showed my aunts how pretty I was in my brand new yellow ao dai and black pants. They just smiled.

After the church service, everyone went to my stepmother's uncle's house, where my new stepmother introduced her family to my father. I clearly remember the beautiful pink ao dai that my stepmother had chosen for the reception. Here was where dad presented her with her dowry, which included a set of gold earrings, a gorgeous necklace, a bracelet, and, of course, the wedding ring which he had given her at the church. We stayed in her uncle's home for that night and then returned to Cu Chi the next morning, bringing my new stepmother home with us.

The celebration continued when we got back to Cu Chi. There was a big party for all our family members and friends along with the priest and the church elders. I have no idea what it cost, but the party had to be an enormous expense. Fortunately, the custom in Vietnam was for the guests to give money to the bride and groom to offset the wedding cost.

After the reception, there wasn't time or money for them to go on a honeymoon. My stepmother simply joined us in our house and participated in our normal activities. She was so young that she seemed more like a big sister than a mother. She was very sweet and didn't speak much. She and I didn't have many problems at all in the beginning. Of course, I was young and didn't yet have any assigned chores like my oldest sister Luyen.

Luyen was a different story. She was now a teenager and had typical teenage problems with authority, especially if that authority was from the woman who *replaced* her *real* mother. The two of them fussed with each other all the time. Their relationship only got worse after my stepmother gave birth to her firstborn, my new sister, Vinh.

Everything Luyen did seemed to upset my stepmom. She would complain if Luyen got new clothes or stayed out too late with friends. As Luyen got older, the tensions between them only increased.

When Luyen turned seventeen, several boys in the village were very interested in her. The fact that my father was a teacher, a position of much honor, made her an excellent match for any worthy boy.

One such prospect was the son of Mr. Nguyen. He had been a low-level bureaucrat at our village in the North but now was a wealthy man in the firework business. The two fathers made the match for a 4,000 dong dowry, paid to my father. They then set a date for the wedding.

When the day occurred, the celebration was huge, the biggest my village had ever seen up to that time. Luyen's fiancé, Do, drove from his home in Xom Moi, about two hours away, in a big, beautiful, black car decorated with fresh flowers. Do was a handsome man, especially in his black suit.

Although my sister was not the most beautiful girl in the village, she was very charming and looked quite fetching in her red ao dai overlayed with a white ao dai. After the wedding, she moved away with her new husband, and I didn't see my sister again for a couple of years.

Now that Luyen was married, our family faced a new reality. We needed more money. Father's teaching salary had not increased even as things had gotten more expensive. Even with Luyen moving out, Vinh had joined our family. He decided that it was time for him to join the rest of the village men in making firecrackers when he was not teaching.

Because he wasn't physically strong enough for much of the work on the larger fireworks, he made phao new or thrown fireworks. These fireworks were small, and about one inch cubed all wrapped in different colors. When someone threw one at the street, it exploded with a big noise.

Making this kind of firework was so safe that my sisters and I could even help. When Dad came home from his day at school, he mixed all the ingredients required for the explosive. Then, after we completed our homework, Phan, and I would go over to Mrs. Kiem's home to assemble them. The work was fun, and I got paid very well. I even made fifty cents more than my sister because I knew that mine was perfect. The best part was that I got to keep all the money I made for myself.

Every night, after dinner, we made the cubes. I enjoyed the work because it allowed me to spend time with my father while making money for the family. While we worked, Father would usually tell us a story.

He was an amazing storyteller. He would tell us ghost stories or maybe one about a girl or boy getting lost in the forest and how their fairy godmother would help them by leading them back home. The tales were all different, but they always had a good moral to them at the end. Some of the stories were so long that he had to continue them the next night. Dad would often pretend to forget where he had left off. We would laugh. We never forgot and would quickly remind him.

We continued in this manner for several years, and we were happy. Then disaster struck. We lost our house. More precisely, the other side of our house where Mr. Su's family lived burned down. With only a wall separating us, the fire ruined most of our stuff as well.

Mr. Su made the other kind of firecrackers, the dangerous ones. One day, while he and his team were working, there was a spark, powder somehow ignited, and his side of the structure burned down.

I had been playing outside with a friend when the big explosion rocked the neighborhood. I was so frightened. I ran to my friend's house, crying because I had no idea if any of my family had survived the blast and fire. I was so relieved when I saw them coming out of our side of the home.

In truth, no one died in the explosion and fire, a miracle in itself. Over the next few days, the Su's moved to Saigon, leaving a burned-out shell where their home used to be. On our side of the wall, the structure was still sound – it just needed some repairs. Unfortunately, most of our clothing, beds, tables, and benches had burned, and we had to replace them.

The greatest loss was some of our family's birth records. These had come from the north, and my father had to refile them here using only my father's memory as a source. Consequently, ages fluctuated as birthdates changed. On a positive note, I gained a new middle name, Thanh. I liked it. My name had always been Van or "cloud." Now it was Thanh Van or "blue cloud", much prettier.

Chapter 3

*"Do not be overcome by evil,
but overcome evil with good."*

(Romans 12:21)

Looking back at my time in Cu Chi, I realized that tragedy was an integral part of life. The fire at the house was only an example of bad things happening in my world. Thankfully, my family was safe, but Mr. Su's family lost everything. Many others in our community suffered as we journeyed through life together.

Ms. Bao was a single woman in our community. Each family had an acre of land, and Ms. Bao's acre was adjacent to ours. Like all our neighbors, we planted cu san on the property line. The plant grew straight and tall, almost providing a privacy fence, and had the additional benefit of having an edible root. Ms. Bao was always friendly and a stalwart member of our local parish. She contributed a lot of money to the church, which she earned by making fireworks, and helped teach the young girls the Flower Offering Ceremony in the month of October honoring the Virgin Mary. I was one of those girls, and I remembered her fondly. All these good things made what happened to her more difficult to understand.

One day, while making fireworks in her kitchen, which was a separate building from her living quarters, an explosion destroyed the kitchen and killed a young man who had been working with her. The event had a tragic effect on Ms. Bao and began her downward spiral into alcoholism.

Ms. Bao had always been a strongly opinionated woman. She would do anything to get her point across. Many evenings, she would sit outside her house with a bottle of ruou de, a Vietnamese rice liquor. As people passed by, she would judge them for any of a thousand different things, often unjustified. If they dared to talk back to her, she would curse them loudly, gathering attention from all around.

I remember when a rumor passed through the village that she was pregnant. She was a single woman, which would have been a terrible disgrace. However, what she did in response was even worse. She took her underwear from her period and mounted it on a pole. She then proudly waved her "flag" in front of those who passed by as proof of her "innocence."

My father, as well as much of the community, was outraged by her actions. He ordered me inside so I couldn't hear what she was shouting at people. Of course, she was a very loud woman, and from what words I could make out, I couldn't believe that she claimed to be a Christian woman and that she used that same mouth to praise God on Sunday!

Around the same time, we had another neighbor, Mr. Nghe, who lived in the home directly in front of ours. He provided for his family by making cha lua, a kind of Vietnamese bologna. He lived in the house with his wife An, his mother, Mrs. Ca, his brother, Nghiem, and his sister, Thai. Theirs was not a happy household.

An's responsibility was to take the finished cha lua to market for sale. On one market day, the money disappeared, either lost or stolen, on the way back to the house. That night, I listened from my window as Mr. Nghe severely beat her for the loss.

I had seen him hit her before, sometimes with the same whip he used on the horses, but this time was far worse. She broke away and ran crying to our front door, where she begged sanctuary, which, of course, my father allowed.

Mr. Nghe followed her and began beating on our door with such ferocity that Father was sure that he was going to break it down. Quickly, he hurried An out the back door, allowing her to run to another house while he tried to calm her husband down.

A few weeks later, Mr. Nghe came to my father and said that An had not come home and would my father draft a report for the police. Since Mr. Nghe did not read or write, my father dutifully wrote down An's description and pertinent information regarding her disappearance. Then he gave the letter to Mr. Nghe to deliver to the police.

Later in the week, another neighbor, Mr. Thoc, wandered over to a neighbor's house looking for a lost chicken. The neighbor had moved, and the house was vacant. He noticed a terrible smell coming from inside. Being curious, he ventured a little farther and made a horrific discovery. He found An's body lying on banana leaves with her neck cut.

He immediately screamed for assistance which got a lot of attention. Since Father was a leader in the community, people came to get him. Since we lived so close to Mr. Nghe, my father was third on the scene with me close on his heels.

Father took charge of the situation, immediately ordering all the people to stay away and, under no circumstances, enter the house. He sent one of the villagers to get the police and then stood guard by the door until they arrived. The police put up yellow tape all around the building while they investigated and searched for the husband, Mr. Nghe. It wasn't long before they found him and took him to the police station. After interrogation, he openly admitted to killing his wife. I felt that going to prison was too good for him.

After the investigation of the murder, the police released Ms. An's body to her mother-in-law, Mrs. Ca, for funeral preparation. In Vietnam, we didn't have funeral homes; the body would be put in a coffin and kept at the deceased person's house for a few days before burial.

Six strong, young men carried her body the short distance from the house where she was found to her home. Now, Chi An was an average person, about one hundred thirty pounds, and shouldn't have been that difficult to carry. Yet, those six young men claimed that the coffin got heavier with each step as they got closer to her house. It was as if she didn't want to come home, even in death.

At night, people from the church would come over to her house to pray for her. We went almost every night, and there would be several other people there as well. One night, An's four-year-old son joined us. As we prayed around the coffin, the boy would look at the corner of the room and say, "my mother stands right there." I heard him say it. Neither I nor anyone else saw her, but we could not sway him from insisting that she was there. Who was I to question him?

Chapter 4

"To sum up,
all of you be harmonious, sympathetic, brotherly,
kindhearted, and humble in spirit; not returning evil for
evil or insult for insult but giving a blessing instead; for
you were called for the very purpose that you might inherit
a blessing."

(1 Peter 3:8-9)

When North and South Vietnam separated in 1954, both parties had agreed that a free election forming a united Vietnam would occur within two years. For many reasons, that election never took place. The North had committed too many infractions against the South and her American allies. There was no way they would allow an election now. The North accused the South of undermining the future of the country. The problem for the South was that the North had anticipated this happening.

Northern infiltrators had remained in South Vietnam since the country's division in 1954. Their job was to nudge the people's thinking toward favoring Ho Chi Minh's government in the North. Now, as the deadline for the election passed and a peaceful resolution to the separation became harder to imagine, their purpose also changed to one of subversion and street warfare.

The North began building supply lines through Cambodia and Laos partly to support the southern revolutionaries in South Vietnam, favoring insurrection against the "corrupt" regime of President Ngo Dinh Diem. Some of these routes, known as the Ho Chi Minh Trail, were partly underground – a complex tunnel system completely hidden from Southern eyes. Some of those tunnels had their terminus at our village of Cu Chi.

My father became aware of these tunnels and the people traveling in them when members of the Viet Cong, southerners supported by the North and strongly against President Diem, came to him for his help. Since he was an educator and a respected member of the Cu Chi community, they wanted his assistance in influencing the people to join their cause and fight for the reunification of Vietnam under Hanoi's rule.

They picked the wrong man to try and influence. There was no way my father could find it in his heart to join with them. Only a few years had passed since we had abandoned all we owned to escape men like these. Compatriots of these men had forced my stepmother to watch her father brutally murdered for perceived crimes against the state. To join in the Communist cause now would be unthinkable, so my father did the opposite.

He traveled to Saigon and joined the South Vietnamese Police. By doing so, he would take a stand and do what he could to support his adopted country. He agreed that the government in the South was less than perfect, but even with the South's faults, he felt their ideas were better than what was happening in Hanoi.

After signing up, they sent him to Saigon to train where he stayed with a friend. He moved the family to Xom Moi where both of my uncles lived, only about thirty minutes from of Saigon instead of the hours it would take from Cu Chi.

We stayed in Xom Moi for about a year while Father trained, and for me, life didn't change much. The physical location was different, but school was school. Now that I was in the fourth grade, new friends replaced the old ones left behind in Cu Chi. My sister Vinh was now four years old, and when I got home from school, she glued herself to my side and went everywhere I went. My sister, Hanh, was born in a few months, a welcome addition to our growing family.

Of course, after giving birth, my stepmother could not be expected to do household chores. Vinh was still too little, so my stepmother's jobs fell to Phan and me. Phan did the cooking while I did the laundry – including a lot, and I mean a lot of dirty diapers.

Remember, this was Vietnam, not the U.S. We had no washing machine and no disposable diapers. We didn't even have running water in the house at this time! We had a well, and every day I would go there, along with all the other women in the community, and draw up the water I needed for the laundry that day. Then I would hand-wash the clothes and diapers and hang them out to dry at the back of our house.

After graduating from the police academy, his

superiors assigned him to a post at a precinct in Bien Hoa, a province about fifteen miles east of Saigon, right across the Dong Nai River. As part of his police salary, the government provided Dad with a half of a room with an addition amounting to another half room in the police compound. These served as living room and formal dining room when we had guests. It was not much, but for the time being, it was ours.

Father reserved one room for him and my stepmother, along with the younger children. I must admit I was a little jealous. I remembered all too well what joy there was being the youngest and getting to sleep with dad and stepmom.

Uncle Ba Hoa helped Father build another room with a tin roof. This served as a bedroom for Phan and me. It also functioned as the living area and kitchen. It was about thirty feet from the main living space.

The kitchen table was not only for eating. Father used it to talk to guests, and Phan and I did our homework there. The house fronted on a swampy area that had an awful, rotten smell to it most of the time. That didn't bother Dad. He constructed an extension over the swamp to give us some additional room. Eventually, we hardly noticed the smell anymore.

In addition to our lives, our schooling was interrupted by our move to Bien Hoa. Public schools in Vietnam did not allow transfers, late, or incomplete enrollees. As a result, I had to finish fourth grade at a local Catholic school before being admitted to the fifth grade in public school.

Phan, who was always drawing something or someone, took an entrance exam to the prestigious art high school – L'Ecole des Arts Applique de Bien Hoa. Her score on the entrance test was the third highest and received a scholarship of 400 dong per semester. I was so happy that she was getting this chance. Although we were going to different schools, hers was located right across the street from mine. I went there often after classes just to peer through the windows searching for her. Her good fortune, however, also had an unfortunate side effect. Her school was full time from eight to twelve in the morning and from two to five in the afternoon; consequently, most of her chores became mine. There seemed to be an unending list of things I had to do at the house.

In addition to washing the clothing for seven people, I also did the ironing, cooking, and hauling water for our personal use. I could never get the knack of balancing water on poles like other women in the compound. Instead, I carried water from the public fountain in ten-gallon containers using only my hands.

As onerous as this task was, it was bearable

during the wet season. The fountain right outside our house provided all we needed. In the dry season, however, that was not the case. The closer fountain dried up. Instead, I had to go to the one outside the main police building, almost three blocks away. I often had to get up at four in the morning to retrieve our daily water supply before school began.

I found little things I could do to make my jobs easier from watching the other women. I had already been washing our clothing at the fountain. Now, since most of the women washed their dishes there as well, I did too. The task of carrying the dishes or clothing back and forth was much less tiring than hauling all that extra water.

People used the fountains for other things too. Both men and women, including me, would take "scoop baths" there. Men would remove their shirts to wash, while women bathed in their clothing. Privacy was not a word heard very often in our community.

By the time I finally finished my chores in the evening, I was often too exhausted to do justice to my schoolwork. As a result, my grades plummeted until I found myself in the middle of the class, which I had never experienced before.

As depressing as this was, I realized that, under the circumstances, my education situation was not likely to improve. I wouldn't say I liked it, but that was how it was going to be. Just because I was doomed to a mediocre position didn't mean it had to be so for the others.

With that in mind, I redoubled my efforts with them, assuring that the four of them, Hanh, Vinh, and later, my brother He, along with Cousin Chinh who was living with us, placed in the top ten of their grades. I carefully watched them do their homework every night.

We continued living in the police station compound for the next five years until I was well into high school. High school is different in Vietnam. Any education after primary school was considered high school – in other words, sixth through twelfth grades. Furthermore, there was no guarantee of attending high school. Each student had to be evaluated and accepted by a school.

Consequently, the end of fifth grade was a stressful time. Every student took a test at the end of the term that determined whether they could continue their education or have to train for a trade. Both private and public high schools used this exam for entrance. Even with my so-so grades, my test went well, and I found myself accepted to Ngo Quyen High School, the only public high school in town.

All schools in Vietnam require uniforms. For girls, the uniform was either a blue or white ao dai. I could wear the blue one only on Mondays while the rest of the week required the white ones. My stepmother provided me with the bare minimum – one blue and two white. I managed with these during the dry season. I remained presentable by washing the dirty one every day, drying it in the sun while I wore the other one to school. The rainy season was a bit different.

The monsoon rains often fell all day, every day, rarely breaking for more than a few minutes. Since I had to walk the two miles to and from school every day, my ao dai would be soaking wet by the time I got home. With the seemingly endless rain, there would be no way for my ao dai could dry in time for the next time I needed it. Since I hated walking to school in a wet ao dai, I needed to improvise.

Phan and I were given two dong (Vietnamese money) every morning for breakfast. We could use it to eat, or we could save it. The decision was ours. Consequently, we went hungry a lot of the time. I kept my money for another ao dai, an extra blouse, or pants – things that were much more important than food! After all, a girl has to do what a girl has to do.

In high school, I discovered another girl who lived on the other side of the compound. Her name was Net, and we became close friends. Although we went to the same school, we didn't take the same classes because of our foreign language courses. My school offered two languages – French and English.

We chose one to study in sixth grade as a second language. I chose French; she chose English. In tenth grade, we picked a third language to learn. Mine was English; Net had French. Consequently, our classes never coincided, although we could still walk to and from school together.

Every night at eight o'clock, after I finished my housework, Net and I went to the coffee shop. Phan and I needed coffee to stay awake to study. On our way, we passed by a small park a few blocks away from my house. The park was almost always busy in the evening. Net and I frequented it often along with her other friends. Even though they never said anything about my clothing, I always felt a little self-conscious around Net and her friends. They usually wore expensive ao dai with fancy needlework, while mine was the cheapest cloth my stepmother could find.

After a few minutes, though, surrounded by their happy laughter, I allowed my awkwardness to pass and would join in with them in their jokes and stories. The park was almost always busy in the evening. Young families, often with small children, walked and played. Most importantly, from our perspective, teenage boys roamed the walkways.

The boys were crude and often made obscene comments when Net and I passed by them. We would properly hold our heads down as if to ignore them while, at the same time, glancing out of the corner of our eyes to see which boys had shown interest. Afterward, we would laugh about the encounter. We knew that this was only the boys' inexperienced way to flirt.

In 1965, my family's fortunes improved immensely when my stepmother took a job working in the mess hall for the U.S. Army at Long Binh. In addition to her salary, the army allowed her to bring home some extra food – Western food. Of course, she never knew what would be available in advance, but that just added to the mystery and the surprise.

She would often bring home such luxuries as hot dogs, bacon, battered chicken, and, best of all, chicken eggs. In Vietnam, only the very rich could afford chicken eggs while the rest of us had to get by with duck eggs – not a worthy substitution at all.

Sometimes, after reassuring ourselves that everyone else in the house was sound asleep upstairs, Phan and I would raid the food cache and prepare a little "midnight snack" guaranteed to carry us through the next morning, saving us two dong!

The downside of my stepmother's windfall was the power that it gave her within the family. Now that she was a provider, she felt equal to my father and even more of an overlord to me. I don't know if she meant to be wicked toward me, but she was.

My workload, already high, increased because she could not do things around the house now that she was working, and, unfortunately, Father agreed with her. Each day after she came home from work, I was required to boil water and prepare a bath for her. Of course, this meant more water for me to haul from the fountains each day.

If her day had not gone particularly well, our stepmother would take it out on Phan and me. She would scream at us, telling us we were lazy, no-good teenagers and that all we were good for was being prostitutes in one of the "houses" near the base.

She wondered aloud why no boys ever came to the house asking to marry us, insinuating that there was something wrong with us. We never told her that we discouraged the boys. We didn't want to marry yet. We knew that would only irritate her more. All we wanted was to finish school and improve our lives. We were smart enough never to imply that removing ourselves from her presence was how we were going to accomplish said self-improvement.

Before my stepmother got the job at the base, I could usually talk to my father about her. He would even intervene on my behalf if he felt she was being unreasonable. Now though, she had more power, and my father had begun listening to her more than me. The tension within the house, already high, had become almost a physical entity of its own. Finally, the stress of dealing with the women in his life got so bad that my father became seriously ill. His doctor had to admit him to the hospital for a week. While he was under care, my two uncles came to the house to speak to us. The constant conflict had to stop. Father's job was already stressful; he did not need the additional stress at home. They begged for us to change. If we didn't, the doctors felt that my father could die.

That revelation did it for me. Even though my attitude was the same, I vowed to change how I responded to my stepmother. She still vexed me with her demands and belittling comments, yet I learned to ignore her cursing and critical words. Whenever I sensed that she was about to unload on me, I prayed for patience and asked God to help me keep my mouth shut and not talk back. I offered my silence as an offering of obedience to God. Overall, this plan worked well for me, and a false semblance of peace existed in our home.

All our neighbors knew about the bad relationship between my stepmother and me. We had been here in the compound for almost five years, and I had many friends among the people there, especially those I talked to at the fountain every morning.

Many women had similar situations at their

houses, and we commiserated over our trials. Several of my Aunts – we often called older women aunts or older men uncles – approached me and let me know that they were free to talk if I wanted.

One of these women, Aunty Ba Hoa, lived next door. She was a beautiful, sweet soul, as was her husband. Between them, they had thirteen children. Even with so many in her house, she would take time for me. No matter how busy she was, she would take me under her wing and would help me when she could.

One thing Aunty Ba Hoa could do better than anyone was cook. Everything she made melted in your mouth. Even with fifteen mouths to feed, she would almost always manage to put a little bit aside for me as well.

Remembering Phan, I would eat half of what I was given and save half for my sister – most of the time. If what Aunty had prepared was particularly delicious, or I was extra hungry, Phan's half didn't quite make it home. I always felt guilty for that later, but I never told Phan about it.

Chapter 5

"The Child continued to grow and become strong, increasing in wisdom; and the grace of God was upon Him."

(Luke 2:40)

When I turned seventeen, my father bought a house away from the compound. I was excited because the new home was much closer to my school than the old house had been. I wouldn't have to walk nearly as far, only about a mile instead of two.

As a bonus, the house was much larger as well. It had a living room, two bedrooms, a kitchen, and – oh joy – a bathroom with a real toilet. No more community bathrooms! Of course, we still slept on the floor, but the house was clean, and we were its only residents. No other families shared walls with us. The place would've been perfect, but for one small detail.

That detail was a house of prostitutes living in the alley between our new home and the main road. Father hadn't realized it when he bought the house because it had been daytime, but the truth became very apparent as evening turned to night.

Of course, prostitution was still illegal in Vietnam. When the police raided the bordello, the girls would run all over trying to get away from them. One night, one of the girls ran to the corner of our house – stark naked. Father was not amused.

Father was now a lieutenant in the police force security division. He and his group were responsible for using intelligence to locate communist cells plotting the country's overthrow. Some of these places were quite respectable; the Communists even used Buddhist temples to cover their actions. Father was decidedly not happy having a bordello just down the street from where his four daughters lived, so he decided to do something about it. He arranged for the street patrols to increase the number and the severity of their raids on the illegal prostitution operation.

The girls who worked there were either arrested or just left in frustration, giving the owner no option but to close. Since Father was a plain-clothed officer, he wore a white shirt and a tie to work. No one in our new neighborhood knew what he did for a living. Consequently, they never discovered who was responsible for cleaning up the area.

Even though our local "house" had been closed, prostitution still ran rampant through the city of Bien Hoa. With a U.S. Air Force base nearby and a U.S. Army post only six miles away at Long Binh, our quiet little city was full of lights and loud music after dark.

There was always a large contingent of American GIs drinking in the bars, along with South Vietnamese soldiers, gang members, and prostitutes. The GIs' oversized military vehicles made the city's narrow streets all but impassable, even for bicycles and pedestrians.

In their search for feminine companionship,

many of the soldiers wandered through the streets. Most of the time, they were drunk, shouting their desires from the tops of their lungs. Because most Vietnamese spoke little to no English, we feared the big foreigners and did our best to stay away from them.

Young women, like myself, found the streets increasingly unfriendly at night and decidedly unsafe. Consequently, my sisters and I stayed home. Traveling outside simply wasn't worth the risk. If there were anything that we must have before morning, He, my brother, would get it for us. In effect, we were prisoners in our own house. Our fear ruled us.

Chapter 6

"Put on the full armor of God, so that you will be able to stand firm against the schemes of the devil."

(Ephesians 6:11)

Even in wartime, time continues to pass, even though it can move almost imperceptibly when sandwiched between battles and bombs. Soon, another year had passed, and it was time for New Year or TET, as we called it. Our New Year was not the western celebration on January 1. The Vietnamese people had based our celebration on the lunar new year for centuries. This year TET began on January 30, 1968. Little did we know how different this new year would be.

Preparation for TET was hard labor, yet a labor of love as well. Father instructed me to clean all the windows, mop the floors, and clean all the pots and pans until they seemed as if they were new. He wanted the whole house to sparkle when the new year came.

Other people in the community went as far as to repaint their homes to ensure that they would have good luck in the New Year. They prayed that the old year's bad luck would run in fear from the firecrackers as they exploded in the streets.

Much of the new year's mystique found its beginnings in Buddhist traditions. Even though cleaning the house was not a Christian practice for New Year, we always did our best to ensure that our home was perfect for receiving the family and friends who would visit during the seven-day celebration.

Most Vietnamese people didn't give presents at Christmas, even among the Christian community, but that changed dramatically at New Year. During the year, my father helped many people both personally and professionally, and this was when they would show their gratitude by bringing him small gifts, often liquor.

My dad didn't drink, but that was no problem. On the second day of the celebration, his brothers always appeared to help him out by dividing all the liquor between them. We children had our traditions too. We would get our books out to study so that the new year would allow us to learn diligently all year long.

The part I loved most about the new year celebration was the clothes. Every year, we got to wear new clothes made especially for the festival. Early in the morning of the first day of TET, we gathered to wish our parents wealth, happiness, prosperity, luck, and health during the new year. They, in turn, would give us "lucky money" that we could spend any way we wanted.

Unfortunately, the new year also meant additional stress at school. As the new year began, I was in the eleventh grade and would have to take the first of two graduation exams required by the state. As always, the stress came from the consequences of not scoring well. If you were a girl, you were fortunate. You could repeat the eleventh grade, find a job, or get married. If you were a boy, however, there was no choice. Your failure meant automatic induction into the military. With the stakes so high, many students would go to night classes or hire a tutor to help guarantee passage.

Hanh Do, a friend of mine from school, had a brother, Anh Tai, who had graciously offered to tutor us. "Anh" translates to brother in English. Since he was Hanh's brother, we all used that title to address him.

Anh Tai was tall, six-foot-two at a minimum, charming, friendly, and incredibly handsome. He attended the university in Saigon during the week and could only work with us on the weekends when he returned home. Because he looked to be an excellent tutor, several of us went up to Hanh's house on the first day of TET to learn from him.

That Friday evening, we gathered to get acquainted with our tutor. Anh Tai spoke up and jokingly asked who the best cook among us was. All my friends immediately pointed to me, saying I was a great cook and an excellent caretaker of my brother and sisters.

I was stunned. How embarrassing! I put up with the nonsense for only an hour when I told them I needed to go home. I created an excuse, saying that my father had only permitted me to be gone for an hour because of the celebrations that evening.

Anh Tai immediately thought that I would be with my boyfriend and confronted me about it. Exasperated and sputtering, I assured him that I did not have a boyfriend. I was firmly committed to my studies, and romance was the last thing on my mind. Phuong told him that I had many admirers. She said that she had once seen two men on a swing just outside my window while cooking.

Anh Tai gave me a questioning look, so I told him the truth. "That was Uncle Uc and his friend Anh Nghia. Yes, they were sitting on the swing, but they were at Uncle Uc's house. Yes, their being there made me feel uncomfortable, but the window had to be open so that I had enough light to see. Neither of them is my boyfriend!"

Frustrated and upset, I once again excused myself from the group and started home. Daylight was turning to night, and my father didn't like it when I was out late. Reluctantly, Phuong, Gai, and Loan also decided to go home with me to walk together.

As we left the house, Hanh ran up to me and said, "You forgot your book!" I didn't understand. I hadn't brought any books here. She had a twinkle in her eye as she thrust the book into my hand. It was the annual New Year publication from Anh Tai's University. Why would he give it to me? A million questions crossed my mind as I took the book and continued walking home, all the while getting questions, looks, and maybe a few titters from my friends.

When the other girls and I parted company, I saw Anh Tai's small Honda motorcycle out of the corner of my eye. I wondered; *Had he been following us?* My heart started beating faster at the thought, and I knew the blood was rushing to my face. Why did he affect me this way? I hardly knew him. Still, the idea that he was interested in me gave me a warm feeling all the way down to my toes. The car crept behind me until I turned into the alley that led to my house. Then, he sped up and drove away.

The experience made me more than a little uncomfortable. I had no prior experience with this type of behavior. Boys had never followed me home! As soon as I got into the house, I rushed upstairs to the room I shared with Phan. I wanted to tell someone, but I wasn't sure who I could tell. I did know that if I spoke with my father, he would become upset. He might even accuse me of openly flirting with strange boys, resulting in a spanking... or worse.

I remembered what had happened to my older sister, Luyen. When Father heard about her boyfriend, a boy that didn't meet his approval, his solution was to marry her off to the first suitable man he could find – which he did. I certainly didn't want that! Marriage was not in my immediate plans, so I decided to keep my mouth shut. If Dad somehow found out... Well, I would deal with that situation later. Questions flew through my mind as I tried to settle into sleep – as if sleep was going to come to me that night.

As I lay on my pallet, pretending to sleep, I was disturbed by a flurry of firecrackers going off—no big deal. We expected lots of fireworks during TET, and the holiday had barely started its seven-day run. Somehow, though, these firecrackers sounded different, more like another sound I knew but couldn't quite remember. All at once, my eyes snapped open, and my heart began to race. What I was hearing was not firecrackers but gunfire – gunfire that was getting closer to our house by the second.

My father shouted out, "The Viet Cong are nearby! We need to go to the sandbag room at once." As its name suggested, our father had lined the sandbag room with sandbags. Supposedly, they would protect us from stray bullets, although it wouldn't do much good against bombs. If a rocket hits the house... Well...at least we would all die together.

I was almost in the room when I remembered that I had left my window open. I realize now that running back upstairs to close it was pretty stupid, but that was what I did. I stood by the open window as rockets flashed across the sky toward Bien Hoa Airbase. I could hear the base's sirens sounding and the reverberation as shells exploded nearby. They were so loud that I thought my eardrums were going to burst. I quickly slammed the window closed and ran back toward the sandbag room. My family and I spent a sleepless night there, huddled together as the sounds of war raged outside.

The next morning an eerie calm filled the city. There were no more explosions or machine gun fire. People on the streets were full of stories about the Viet Cong raid of the previous evening. Timed as it was, the enemy's attack initially caught the American and South Vietnamese forces off-guard.

Both sides had agreed to a TET ceasefire. The troops had expected a lull in the fighting, not a shock attack. The North, however, showed again that it was not to be trusted. They had entered the agreement knowing that they would invade and take their enemies by surprise.

My sister, Phan, and I left the house that morning and wandered around the city, observing the damage that the attack had inflicted as we looked for friends in the crowds. We didn't ask permission of Father because we knew he wouldn't approve. Besides, he would be far too busy with his policing this morning. The attack indicated a fatal flaw in the South's intelligence-gathering capability.

Some people in the neighborhood told Phan and me rumors that the train station had taken a lot of damage, so we went there first. We were surprised. There wasn't much damage to the structure, but we saw several dead bodies – Viet Cong bodies, lying where soldiers had shot them in the streets surrounding it.

I remember thinking that they were so pale, so young, yet, even in death, they looked evil. They represented a regime that had already damaged my family enough. A chill came over me. A glance between my sister and me said she felt it as well. We decided that a war-torn street was no place for us. We didn't belong here.

After I got home, I buried myself in my work, washing the windows at the front of the house. That was when I noticed a now-familiar car passing slowly back and forth across the alley entrance to the neighborhood. Its presence took me off guard. I had never seen Anh Tai drive his car in my area before last night and couldn't imagine what would draw him here now. He passed back and forth several times before leaving abruptly.

Later that day, Anh Tai returned with my friend Hanh by his side to safeguard my reputation. He wanted to explain in person what had happened the night before. Anh Tai had become worried that our group would have problems on the way home, so he followed us. Once he saw us safely into our neighborhood, he attempted to go to his home in Tan Vang. As he approached the bridge, soldiers stopped him at a checkpoint. There had been reports of Viet Cong in Tan Vang and that if he crossed the bridge, they couldn't guarantee his safety.

At that point, Anh Tai chastised himself for not returning home immediately after the class had adjourned. If he hadn't followed us home, he would've been home long before the fighting had started. Still, he knew that he would've done nothing differently – he was glad that he got me home safely. He thanked the soldiers and made his way home, where he also had difficulty finding sleep amid the bombs and gunfire.

A warm feeling came over me at the thought of this handsome young man risking himself so that I could be safe, but naturally, I said nothing to him. We continued to talk about little things, trivial things, things that young people talk about when they aren't sure of what to say. We talked about the foods from the North that I prepared for my family. He talked about his university and Saigon. Somehow, the conversation always returned to what had happened the previous night.

He told me that the radio had announced that

what happened to us had happened all over the country. Over one hundred towns and cities, including thirty-six of the forty-four provincial capitals, were attacked by over 80,000 North Vietnamese and Viet Cong forces. The report called it the largest military operation of the war by either side. Fortunately for us, the attack had been launched prematurely, allowing the South and her allies to rally their defenses. They beat back the northern troops and inflicted heavy casualties on them.

I told him about Phan's and my observations at the train depot that morning. Since then, officials had announced that all schools were to remain closed for two months while all the male teachers took defensive training to defend the schools better after they restarted.

I told Tai I was concerned because this was my eleventh year, and I would have to take the first exam. I was afraid that I wouldn't have enough time to prepare. After I said it, I realized how trivial that would sound after going through a night like last night. He laughed and assured me that everything would be alright.

When we finally ran out of things to say, he politely asked when it would be convenient for him to call on me. I shyly told him that my only free time was Friday or Saturday mornings between eight and ten. Schoolwork, housework, and taking care of my family took the rest of my time.

After that day, I didn't see Anh Tai for several weeks. I had expected to find him at Hanh Do's house when I went there for tutoring the next Friday, but instead, Anh Dung was doing the job in his place. Eventually, Anh Tai and I reconnected on Saturday morning in my living area with my cousin and siblings listening in from the next room. Since they were there, I was very careful about what I said to Anh Tai. We met off and on over the next six months.

Neither of us ever expressed love for the other, but there was no doubt of our feelings. We joked back and forth about our lives. He told me that he enjoyed going out with friends for a drink. I told him that was fine – just make sure they were male friends. We laughed. Everything was wonderful. Despite the war, I was happy.

One day, though, he came to see me with fire in his eyes. His hands shook with anger when he spoke. "Why did you lie to me?" he shouted. "You had a boyfriend after all – Nghia! Are you such a good liar because you come from up north?"

His attack took me by surprise. I told him that Nghia liked me a lot – had told me so, but I never returned his affections and certainly did not consider him my boyfriend. He had written me a letter explaining that he had failed his high school exam and had already received notice to report to the army. He dreaded military service, where he felt certain he would die. His one wish was that I would go out to dinner with him at a restaurant of my choosing.

I was conflicted by his request. I didn't love him at all. Still, to my naïve mind, the thought of him dying with only this one unanswered wish was too much. I would feel eternally guilty if he died with this one wish in his heart. I agreed to go out with him, but I insisted that Phan come too.

Nothing I said mattered to Anh Tai. He didn't believe me. I knew that I was completely innocent of duplicity, but he didn't care. He left in a rage, leaving me crying in front of my house. When he finally returned two weeks later to beg my forgiveness, I instructed my sister to tell him I wasn't home. He had hurt me so badly by his words that I couldn't bear to see him. I had never had my birth in the North thrown at me that way, and it stung coming from someone I held dear. In my heart, I knew that it was over between us.

A few months later, I heard gossip that he had a new girlfriend. The rumors said she had moved in with him and was pregnant with his child. They remained unmarried, a terrible disgrace for the girl. I remembered one time while we were still a couple. He asked me why I didn't want to get married. I told him that it was my decision and none of his business.

No one was going to force me into it. Besides, I was not ready for that kind of relationship – not then.

Chapter 7

"Let no one look down on your youthfulness, but rather in speech, conduct, love, faith and purity, show yourself an example of those who believe."

(1 Timothy 4:12)

High school came and went. I graduated in 1970, a little older than some, but wiser because of it. Phan had been working for the US Air Force as an interpreter on Bien Hoa Airbase. On Sundays she volunteered with Father Major James Cain in his civic action work with the Bien Hoa orphanage. He helped her to gain acceptance to Lamson Business College, a private school in Phoenix Arizona. She left Vietnam in August 1969.

After she left, I was virtually alone. I realized that advanced study was not happening for me. My stepmother would not support me to further my education. If I continued, it would be all up to me. My future was in my hands.

My dream was to become a dentist, and I knew that I had to get a job to pay my tuition for my goal ever to happen. Fortunately, the war had created many jobs for those bright enough to seek them out and work them. I quickly found employment with the U.S. Army as a salesclerk in the commissary.

After only a few months, my supervisor discovered my mathematical skills, which landed me a better job in the accounting office. I became solely responsible for calculating the daily sales report, a huge task. The commissary made a lot of money – sometimes $10,000 in a single day. Now, $10,000 was a huge amount in 1970, where $100 would be a house payment back in the States.

Being fresh out of high school, I didn't have any real work clothes. Consequently, I still wore the same ao dai that I had worn to school every day. I couldn't wait for my first paycheck, which I had decided to dedicate to updating my wardrobe other than the money I gave my father to help with family expenses. After all, I wanted to show him that I was a responsible person, an adult in my own right.

My job in accounting led me to a still better one with Suoi Cat Long Binh, a part of the commissary that dealt with wholesale liquor, beer, and soda sales to bars all over Vietnam. It was a huge place with a large yard surrounded by a tall fence with barbed wire at the top. There were four offices within the compound. I shared one of them with my friend Chen while another housed the cashiers, including Nguyen, another friend.

I never intended to date an American. My father would never have allowed it. The shame to the family would be too great. Nonetheless, some of my friends did. One day, Nguyen asked me to eat with her and her boyfriend. In Vietnam, it was customary for a single woman to take a friend along on a date to protect her reputation.

I had gone with Nguyen and her boyfriend, a captain in the army, several times. I told her I would be happy to go again but wondered if her boyfriend could bring a friend for me, so I didn't feel so out of place. He never complained, but I felt awkward asking him to pay for my meal every time. Nguyen's friend agreed to bring someone along. The friend he got was Shady.

Shady, yes, that was his real name, was several years older than the captain's twenty-five years, but he was still somewhat attractive and seemed nice enough. He was not in the army; he was a civilian working for the U.S. Department of Defense. We had a nice time at dinner, and then Nguyen and I went home.

The next day at the office, I asked her, "Why did you introduce me to an old man?" She sat smiling and said, "I don't remember you complaining when you ate all the food he bought!" I grinned as I replied, "Well, he was nice but just a little too old for me."

Regardless of my initial feelings about him, Shady seemed to like me. He had given me his telephone number and told me to call him at any time. He said he would be in my office within five minutes whenever I called.

I was confused. I didn't know what to think. Looking back on the evening, I never gave Shady any indication that I was interested in him. After all, dating an American had never been my goal. There were several reasons for this. The most important being that I felt that my English was too poor. Now, faced with an American admirer, I wasn't sure how to continue.

I began bringing a book in English that I read at lunch to improve my vocabulary during my downtime. My boss, the master sergeant in charge of the warehouse, didn't seem to mind at all. Whenever I found a word I couldn't pronounce, he was more than happy to explain it to me. He even offered to help me when I got stuck.

I found phrases like "thank you for the invitation" and "lunch was very good" in the book, along with other useful words. Armed with my new knowledge, I hesitantly called Shady and told him that "lunch was very good" and "thank you for the invitation." He laughed and asked if he could come by my office tomorrow and take me to lunch. I said, "Yes."

About the same time, I met another American, Michael. He worked for the CIA and spoke Vietnamese well. I found his job exciting, and he was much closer to my age. He and I went out several times, but the relationship didn't go very far. I decided that I didn't love him, and I doubted that he had any serious feelings for me either.

The day he returned to the United States in 1971, he gave me his address and phone number – just in case. I took them but was smart enough to realize that I would probably never see or speak to him again.

After Michael went home, my relationship with Shady began to blossom. He came to see me practically every day for the next four months. One day, he invited me to accompany him to a party at his friend Mike's house in Bien Hoa. A party with a lot of people sounded fun, so I agreed. I was surprised to discover that Mike's house was only a short distance from the home of one of my high school girlfriends.

I was worried that my friend might see me going out with an American. In my mind, she would tell her mother, who would tell someone else. Eventually, the word would reach my father, who would not understand at all. In his mind, good Vietnamese girls did not date Americans – period.

Americans had earned a bad reputation because most local Vietnamese only encountered the young GIs that frequented the bars and whorehouses in the town. This stigma then tainted the prestige of the older, more mature soldiers and officers.

The malignment of Americans resulted in most girls who dated them being uneducated, often from the country, or previously married and on the prowl. That night, after we got to the party, Shady introduced me to the other Americans and their dates. It didn't take long for me to realize that even though I only had a high school education, I was a genius compared to the other ladies there.

A few weeks after that night, Shady rented a house in Tam Hiep and invited me to live with him there. I said no, which I don't think he expected. I told him that I was not one of his friend's girls. I wouldn't dream of staying with him unless we were married, and before that could happen, he had to have the permission of my father and my two uncles.

Shady said nothing more about the matter until a few weeks later. Out of the blue, he asked if he could come and visit my family. I was startled. His question took me completely by surprise and filled me with dread. I had no idea what to say in response, so I stalled. I said I would have to ask my father first, telling Shady what he said in the morning.

That evening, after my stepmother had gone to bed, I sat down and talked to my father. I demurely asked if my boss could come to visit. He wanted to meet my family. My ruse did not fool my father at all. His response was, "Your boss is OK, but you better not have an American boyfriend." My heart sank. I was doomed.

My saving grace turned out to be my limited grasp of languages. Little as it was, my English far surpassed my father's. He spoke Vietnamese and French, and Shady could only converse in English. I was the only one who could translate, which put me in a unique position for controlling the conversation.

When we sat down to talk, I might not have accurately communicated everything that the two of them said. Instead, I told the two of them what they wanted to hear. Everyone left the gathering smiling and happy. I felt that this first meeting went very well indeed.

The next week, my family invited Shady over for dinner. I made egg rolls, fried rice, and beef stir-fry with vegetables. Shady brought over some soda for my dad since I had told him that Dad didn't drink alcohol. That meeting also went well, resulting in Shady coming over more often. Sometimes, he took me to the movies along with my brother and sisters, of course.

Each time we went out, I was very self-conscious of everyone looking at me. I always wore large dark glasses to shield my identity from the prying eyes of people who might know me. I knew it was wrong to be embarrassed by my relationship with Shady, but I couldn't help it. However, my ruse didn't help me with the people who saw us on the street. The men's comments were the worst, but even little children would shout obscenities at us. It was so hard to smile and wave back at them. I was so happy that Shady didn't speak Vietnamese.

Late in 1971, Shady asked me to marry him. His offer took me completely off-guard. My stuttering response was that I had to ask my father, which I did that evening. To put it mildly, Dad didn't take it very well. His response wasn't a shouting match. Truthfully, he didn't say anything at first, but his disapproval was apparent in his face and the dark cloud that seemed to hang over him the rest of the evening. After a time, he just walked away. As he wandered off, muttering something about having to visit with my uncles.

That last statement should have set off blaring alarms in my head. A few days later, as I came home from work, I found my brother, He, waiting for me where the alley met the main street. He advised me that both of our uncles were at the house waiting for me to get home. They intended to kidnap me and take me to their place to marry a Vietnamese man.

The man they had chosen did business with my Uncle Thuoc. His parents had promised to provide a house on the market if I agreed to marry him. I quickly thanked my brother and sent him home. He was to tell my father that I had not appeared that evening. After my close call, I went to a friend's house. I knew she would let me stay with her for the night.

When I explained what was going on to my friend, Kim, she was more than willing to help me out. Even better, she was my size, so I had clean clothes to wear to work the next day instead of the ones I had worn before.

Shady took me to lunch, where I told him what had happened at home. I was distraught. I loved Shady, and my voice quivered as tears rolled down my cheeks. I looked into his eyes and told him that if

I couldn't marry him, I wouldn't marry anyone and that I would say the same thing to my father. That night I told my father the same thing. His only response was to ask where I had spent the night.

A few days later, my sister Luyen and her husband came from Saigon to meet with my dad and me. Since she was the victim of an arranged marriage, I had thought that she would understand my situation. She didn't. "The solution to your problem was simple," she said, "Shady would have to buy Dad a house and a car to get Dad's permission for the marriage to continue." I couldn't believe what I was hearing.

What was this even supposed to mean? I was so angry! I was not a prostitute! I would never demean myself to that level by demanding payment for Shady's intentions. I loved him, only him. During my rant, my father just sat there, not saying anything. I couldn't believe he didn't intervene. When I finished, I stomped out of the room, leaving them slack-jawed around the table. I never talked to Luyen again after that day.

Next, my stepmother came and pulled me aside. She told me that I should reconsider what my sister had suggested. She knew of another Vietnamese girl who had married an American, and he had bought a house and car for her family. The amount wasn't that much. She suggested that I at least talk to Shady about it.

I wouldn't hear of it. I let her know that I loved Shady for who he was, not his money. I would not cheapen our feelings for one another with such talk. Besides, I knew for a fact that he had little wealth. A large portion of his salary went to his ex-wife for child support and alimony after his divorce.

After finishing with my family, I was so upset that I wrote to the one person I felt I could turn to at this time, my sister Phan in the United States. Then I waited. International mail service was never very fast, but now it seemed interminable as I checked the post daily for her response.

Even though our correspondence took weeks, her words inspired me to act. She suggested that I get a student visa to the U.S. She claimed that once I was on American soil, no one could stop me from marrying Shady. Father's objections would not matter in the least.

Immediately, I began completing the paperwork for the visa. I told Shady, of course, but no one else. I was careful to keep quiet among family and friends. If I had my way, they wouldn't find out until I was on my way to the airport.

The paperwork was long and required many steps as I went through getting signatures and recommendations. The process was a long one and would take months to complete. In the meantime, my sister and stepmother were taking a different path. They decided they would get me to marry someone of their choosing – by any means possible.

Voodoo had come to Vietnam with the French back in the late 1800s and found a home among the more superstitious Vietnamese people. Luyen inquired around and found someone who practiced it in Saigon. She purchased a voodoo spell from the woman that she claimed would force me to change my mind about Shady and make me more agreeable to a different match. As proof that you shouldn't mess with things you don't understand, their plan backfired.

While waiting for the right time to spring the voodoo on me, my stepmother hid it in her closet and subsequently became very ill. She never had a particularly stable personality, but now she acted like a crazy woman, ranting and raving as she wandered around the house and the village's streets.

Her wild eyes and piercing screams petrified her daughters, Vinh and Hanh. Even in her worst moments over the years, she wouldn't have yelled the profanity she was now – especially around the children.

Many years later, my family told me that one night while she was at the funeral for a neighbor, she began speaking in the dead woman's voice. My father performed a sort of exorcism by sprinkling her with holy water. Then he commanded the evil spirit in her body to leave her in the name of Jesus. Eventually, the truth came out. She admitted that the voodoo was a bad idea and put it in the trash. In the meantime, my secret plans to go to the United States continued forward as planned.

Chapter 8

"But an hour is coming, and now is, when the true worshipers will worship the Father in spirit and truth; for such people the Father seeks to be His worshipers. 24 "God is spirit, and those who worship Him must worship in spirit and truth."

(John 4:23)

In February of 1973, my world as I knew it stopped. Shady's work in Vietnam was over, and the Defense Department was reassigning him to stateside work. Only a month had passed since the Paris Peace Accord had officially ended the conflict that kept America here, yet the United States seemed to be in a hurry to get the lion's share of their troops and civilians back home.

I had realized that this day would come; I was just hoping that it would be "later." Why couldn't it have waited for my visa application to be approved? That way we could go together. Unfortunately, my paperwork was still in channels pending further approvals.

Shady had been offered a job at Warner Robbins AFB in Macon, Georgia, where he had begun his civilian career many years ago. This was great news for him. Returning to his hometown where his children lived would be great. I knew how much he loved them. However, the idea that he would see his ex-wife again terrified me. What if he found he still cared for her? What if he remarried her?

When it came time to tell Shady goodbye, I was in a terrible state. I was so distraught that tears ran down my cheeks like rivers, and I could hardly say anything through my sobs. I took his hand before he left and told him, "Once you are back home, you will be around your ex-wife and children again. If you decide to get back with her for the sake of your children, I will understand."

He assured me that nothing would change his mind about us and our future together. He wanted nothing more than to spend the rest of his life with me. His greatest concern was that I might have second thoughts in his absence and decide to stay in Vietnam! When it was finally time to go, he gave me the address and phone number of a mutual friend, Mr. Nakazato, who lived in California. Shady didn't have an address yet in Georgia.

I loved and trusted Shady so much that his words didn't bother me at all. I could not imagine a life without him. I knew that I would wait until we could finally be together in America.

With the loss of the American GIs, the base closed, and I lost my employment as well. I looked for another job for a while, but I found it hard to find anything since my visa and subsequent departure were imminent. No one wanted to hire someone who would be leaving soon. Besides, with the closing of the bases, many Vietnamese were looking for jobs right now.

I was fortunate to find a tutoring job with my friend, Nhung. Nhung had married an American GI and was getting visas for herself and her children. The two of them had a child together plus a daughter from a previous marriage. Phuong, her oldest daughter, was ten years old. She was the one who needed help with her English, and I needed the work.

Phuong and I worked on improving her English for a few months until I received my final approval. I will never forget the first time I came to Nhung's house. As she showed me around, she told me never to touch any of the plants there. She used them to prepare voodoo spells for customers throughout Bien Hoa. Even though Nhung and her husband were very nice to me, I was glad to leave. I remembered all too well my family's recent experience with voodoo and wanted nothing to do with any of her plants.

My visa in my hand, the time had come to say goodbye. I explained to my dad that I was going to the U.S. to continue my studies with Phan. Dad didn't react at all. I think I hurt his feelings when I defied him and said I wouldn't marry anyone if I couldn't marry Shady. I also thought that he suspected the real reason I was leaving, but since he never said anything. I didn't either. Things had not been that good between us for a long time, and I didn't want to make matters worse as I left.

On July 10, 1973, I made my way to the airport in Saigon. I made my goodbyes at home. Vinh, Hanh, and He were sad that I was leaving and wanted to come to the airport with me. I knew that my father and stepmother wouldn't want to bring them, and I knew they were far too young to make their way home alone. I gently told them that our parents needed them here. I promised that I would write to them as soon as I got to America. I felt bad that they couldn't come – that no one came. I could still remember when Phan left to begin her adventure. We all went to see her off, including my two uncles.

Completing the visa paperwork had been tedious but doable. Making travel arrangements hadn't been all that complicated. The idea of flying, however, absolutely terrified me. Other than the trip to the South when I was four, I had never flown before. I couldn't understand how the plane became airborne, let alone what kept it in the air. What if the plane crashed into the ocean and I died – never seeing Shady again? My English was getting better but still heavily accented. Communicating with native English speakers was, at the very least, challenging. I hoped that the people I tried to speak with wouldn't laugh at my accent and make fun of my poor grammar.

As the plane took off, I opened my eyes long enough to take one last look at my country. Even though Vietnam was poor, and life was hard, I found that I loved my country more than ever at that moment. I couldn't believe that the old wood house and banana trees were now so important to me. I secretly wondered what would happen if I never came back. What if I never saw any of my family again? I burst into tears as the thought came and went as the plane continued its long voyage to the east.

My first stop was in San Francisco, which was also the first test of my passport and visa. I was very frightened as I stepped up to passport control and presented my papers. The man was nice and polite, slowing his speech so I could understand what he needed. At the customs table, the officer gave my belongings a cursory examination before allowing me to go to my connecting flight to Phoenix.

The passenger terminal was a swirling mass of humanity. People were going in every direction possible, and I grew disoriented more than once. I was afraid I might miss my flight until a kind person pointed me toward the correct gate.

When I got off the plane in Phoenix, I was elated to see Phan and her husband in the crowd waiting for me. I hadn't realized how tense I was until the relief of that moment washed over me in waves.

The airport in Phoenix was gorgeous. Everything was so clean, so perfect. When we walked out into the parking lot, my astonishment only grew. All the people dressed so nicely, and the parking lot held more cars than I could imagine in the world, let alone one place.

Everything seemed so alien, so different than back home. In my insecurity, I reached for Phan's hand for reassurance like I had done so many times back home. She gently pulled her hand away from mine as she told me that two girls didn't hold hands in America. Doing so suggested something romantic between them, and that was not appropriate. I didn't understand, but I didn't take her hand again.

As we drove to their house, I saw gigantic homes nestled in the mountain valleys. So much space for only one home! Then we passed through a different neighborhood – a poor one. Small wood-frame houses sat almost on top of each other. I was confused. How could this be? I asked Phan, "How could people in the United States be so poor? Wasn't education free, and weren't jobs plentiful?" She told me that not everyone wanted to get an education, and some didn't want to work either. I didn't understand. How could they improve their lot in life without these things?

Phan's house wasn't very big, but it was much larger than ours had been back home. She and I talked incessantly in Vietnamese, hardly stopping long enough to breathe. Her husband, David, had a problem with that. He only spoke English, and I think he felt left out. He and Phan argued quite a bit, mostly about me, I believe. I didn't believe that he wanted me to live with them.

Every morning, the two of them went to school from early in the morning until late in the afternoon, so I had the house all alone. Phan had given me a nice room where I would lie on the bed and listen to the silence. I was astounded at how quiet it was. I never realized how attuned I had become to bombs, gunfire, and sirens until they weren't around all the time. What should have been peaceful was more than a little unnerving.

The only drawback to staying with my sister, other than my brother-in-law's resentment, was that they didn't go to church. I had been a faithful, practicing Catholic my entire life, and I was not ready to let go of my faith. Unfortunately, I had no way to get to the church on Sundays. I was depended on Phan and David to get me anywhere I needed to go. I prayed for guidance, and God intervened in the form of a Mr. and Mrs. Wilson, as God often does.

Mr. Wilson was a member of the Pentecostal Church from Bakersfield, California. He was making the rounds in our neighborhood, inviting people to attend a revival starting that Sunday where his son-in-law was preaching. I explained that I would love to come but had no way to get there. He assured me that would not be a problem. One of the young men from the church would come to pick me up.

I could not do this. My upbringing intervened.

Even in this country where it was commonplace, I was not ready to be seen alone with a young man without a chaperone. I told Mr. Wilson that I would only attend if he and his wife picked me up. He agreed.

That Sunday, the two of them showed up at our door. I was so happy to go to worship, even if it was not the kind I had known in Vietnam. They introduced me to their daughter, Gloria, and their son-in-law, Pastor Mike, the evangelist for the revival. They seemed so happy that I could come. I had no idea what a revival was, but I was so pleased being among Christian believers again that I heartily agreed with everything they said.

I attended the four days of the revival with them, and I felt that I knew them fairly well, and they knew me by the time it was over. I also found that I loved their spirit and zeal for Christ. As we parted, they told me that I was welcome to visit them if I was ever in Bakersfield, California, where they lived. I thanked them for the invitation but didn't think I would ever make it out that way. I didn't know at the time, but God had plans for the Wilsons and me.

Figure 1-1
Those that stayed behind
Van with her family that remained in the north in front of the home where she was born.

Figure 1-2
Van's Mother's burial site in Tu Chau

Figure 1-3
Van outside house where she was born in Tu Chau

Figure 1-4
Inside Tu Chau house. Pictures are of four brothers
Left to right: Nguyen Giao Huan (Van's father), Nguyen Kim Tac (given house when Van's family left); Nguyen Huu Chung, Nguyen Huy Thuoc

Figure 1-5
Parish Church in Tu Chau

Figure 1-6
The house at the police station looking into Van and Phan's room.
Front row: Hanh and He
Back row: Vinh and Van

Figure 1-7
House father purchased in Bien Hoa
Front row: He and Hanh
Back row: Van and a cousin

Figure 1-8

Back Row
Nguyen thi Phan (Phan). b. 1946
Nguyen thi Thanh Van (Van) b. 1950
Nguyen Gia He (He) b. 1962
Hoang thi Noi (Noi) stepmother
Nguyen Giao Huan (Huan) father

Front row:
Nguyen thi Vinh
Nguyen thi Hong Hanh (Tracy) b. 1959

Figure 1-9
Vinh, He, and Hanh going to school

Figure 1-10
A party with friends in Bien Hoa

Figure 1-11
Van in high school

Figure 1-12
Class picture, Van is front row right

Figure 1-13
High school picture
From right: Teacher, Van, friend Hanh, Ha, and Hanh

Figure 1-14
Van at Dong Nai River Park

Figure 1-15
Van working at Suoi Cat Plantation (U.S. Army Base)

Figure 1-16
Van at Suoi Cat Plantation

My Second Life - America

Chapter 9

"For I am afraid that perhaps when I come I may find you to be not what I wish and may be found by you to be not what you wish; that perhaps there will be strife, jealousy, angry tempers, disputes, slanders, gossip, arrogance, disturbances"

(2 Corinthians 12:20)

I had barely unpacked at Phan's house before asking if I could call Mr. Nakazato, Shady's friend. Long ago, he and his wife had been my neighbors before they had immigrated to America. We chatted back and forth about my coming to America and how happy he was that I had come. He said that he didn't have Shady's home phone number but knew how to contact him at work. He promised to do so the very next day.

The next day, my heart leaped in my chest when I heard Shady's voice on the phone. I was beside myself with joy. Shady said he would arrange for a plane ticket to bring me to Georgia as soon as possible. I told him that he had better hurry. I only had six months on my visa.

While I waited for Shady to send me the ticket, my brother-in-law told a friend of his about me, and the two of them arranged a double date. We went bowling which, considering my small stature and the ball's weight, was probably not the best choice. I needed both hands just to pick the ball up. Sending it down the alley was an entirely different problem. Still, we had fun, and the pizza we had afterward was delicious. A few days later, he called me and asked me out. I told him that I couldn't go with him. Someone else owned my heart.

By the beginning of the next week, the ticket finally arrived in the mail. My departure was the next

Saturday! I couldn't believe it; I was going to see Shady again.

Phan and David took me to the airport. Even though I was giddy with anticipation, I was also sad. I didn't know when I would get back to Phoenix, and I would miss Phan terribly – more so since we had so recently reconnected. We had not seen each other for four years. The five weeks we had just shared didn't seem like nearly enough time to make up for the time apart.

I remember stepping off the plane in Atlanta vividly. I saw Shady waving toward me. I could hardly control my joy – until I saw the lady standing next to him. I felt as though someone had plunged a knife into my heart. There was no question but that the lady was his wife, Linda. My fears were confirmed when he introduced us as wife and fiancé.

How cruel! I felt my world collapsing around me, yet what could I say? On the other hand, Linda was crying and screaming a lot and was beginning to gather attention from the others in the airport, so Shady hustled us out to his car where we could talk.

I stumbled through my words as I told him that since he remarried, all I asked was he help support me for a short time while I continued studying English and for assistance in extending my visa. Shady said that he would be more than happy to do that. He drove me to a hotel where I would spend the night.

As soon as I got into my room, my façade melted away. I collapsed onto the bed in tears. The sadness and anger that I had been holding inside came out all at once. I realized at that moment that there was more than one way to die. One was physical death. The other killed the spirit, the soul of the person. That night I was certain that dying in spirit was the worse of the two.

I really couldn't blame them for getting back together. I had told Shady that would be OK! Still, despite seeing them together, I couldn't believe that Shady had remarried her. I really couldn't believe that he had brought me to Atlanta without giving me a chance to back out gracefully. Had he offered me a simple warning, I could have saved face and stayed away.

Was this the same man who had worried that I would change my mind and stay in Vietnam? I had left everything I held close to come to America – to him. I had lied to my father, and the guilt from that deception came back to haunt me now as I wallowed in my misery.

The next morning, Shady arrived at the hotel alone. I was thankful for that, at least. I didn't think I could handle Linda's hysteria again this morning. I assumed he was taking me back to the airport, but he asked to introduce me to his sister in Alabama, a few hours away.

I don't know if it was the shock from the previous day or the fact that I secretly didn't want to leave him just yet. Whatever the reason, I agreed to go. As it turned out, his sister was quite sweet, and we had a wonderful visit. She told me that Shady had talked about me all the time and that she had been dying to meet me. That night, I slept in a room with her two children before Shady and I returned to Atlanta the next day.

The first thing Shady did when we got back was to call the immigration office in Atlanta. Unfortunately, they were closed that week. He swore to get my paperwork in order and forward my green card later.

Despite how wonderful it felt to be with Shady, I realized that I needed to leave here sooner rather than later. After all, he was a married man now, and I wouldn't want to interfere with his relationship with his wife any more than I had. Besides, the longer I was near him, the old feelings I had were bound to come out. I couldn't bear for that to happen.

I needed to go somewhere – but where? If I went back with Phan, the arguments between her and her husband about me would start up again. Besides, I desperately needed God in my life, especially now, and I knew that my sister wouldn't support me in that effort. I remembered the address and phone number that Mr. Wilson gave me. I fumbled in my bag until I found it. As the phone rang, I prayed a silent prayer.

I couldn't believe my luck when Mr. Wilson told me they would be delighted to host me at their home in California. Shady was curious about who Mr. Wilson was. I told him about the Wilsons and reminded him that he had no say in what I did anymore. I could see whomever I wanted. He reluctantly purchased a ticket to Los Angeles the next morning. I maintained a stoic expression and said nothing on the way to the airport. I swore to myself that I wouldn't cry – not here, not now, not in front of him.

I still couldn't believe that the man I had trusted so much had betrayed me. I'd come to Atlanta in the belief that we would have forever. Now, after only a few days, I was vowing never to see or speak to him again. As I walked up the steps to the airplane door, I looked back one last time and waved goodbye to Shady forever.

Chapter 10

"Though youths grow weary and tired,
And vigorous young men stumble badly,
Yet those who wait for the LORD will gain new strength;
They will mount up with wings like eagles,
They will run and not get tired,
They will walk and not become weary."

(Isaiah 40:30-31)

It was a long way from Atlanta to Los Angeles, maybe not as long as the trip from Vietnam in hours, but an eternity longer in my mind. The flight gave me lots of time to think about my life and the new direction it was taking. I thought about my father and the lies I had told him about Shady being my boss.

I was a sinner and deserved all that was happening in my life. I traveled halfway around the world to meet a man who betrayed my trust, and now I was going across the continent to stay with people I had met for a few days months ago. I wasn't even sure I could recognize them. Sounds funny, but all Americans look alike to me!

What if they turned out to be murderers or something equally despicable? I knew no one else in California, so I had no fallback position. Besides my sister and her husband, I knew hardly anyone in America.

Sometime during the flight, as my mind overflowed with turmoil, a hint of peace entered my heart. I remembered that I had trusted in God all along. He had stood by my side all the way, and that helped me realize that God had sent the Wilsons to me as well. I hadn't known that Shady remarried, but God had. I knew that he wouldn't let me down now.

Sure enough, when I arrived at the airport, the Wilsons were waving and cheering as I got off the plane. My insecure heart was pounding as we hugged and walked toward the car. God had not left me alone.

Mr. Wilson loaded us into his late-model Cadillac and drove to their home in Bakersfield, a city about two hours north of Los Angeles. All around me were elaborate houses with lots of land surrounding them. How many wealthy people are there in America to afford such palaces? The Wilsons' house was large too, with a swimming pool between the main building and a trailer at the back of the lot where Mrs. Wilson's parents lived.

As the car pulled up to the door, two young boys came bouncing out of the house to greet us. Nathan was about eight, while Johnny was closer to five. I discovered that the Wilsons had another grown son, Ronnie, who lived with his wife in another home. Mrs. Wilson, Bobbie, told me that they would be over for dinner and bring their daughter, Rebecca.

Bobbie and Beeler, Mr. Wilson's first name, loved their daughter, Gloria. She was gorgeous in body and spirit. Her husband, Pastor Mike, was a gifted speaker. I couldn't understand everything he said, but the way he said it – the power in his voice – set fire to my heart. The church lit up when he spoke about Jesus and the scriptures. Gloria would call every Sunday night to tell her parents about his service that day and how many people the Lord had saved through her husband's preaching.

Occasionally, when she visited her parents, Gloria would take me downtown. There, we would shop for hours in second-hand stores looking for bargains and laughing like crazy people. I had so much fun when we were together. I felt as though I had another sister.

That first night in their home, I did my best to help prepare the dinner. Everything in Bobbie's kitchen was strange to me, so all I could do was wash the vegetables and marvel at the miracles around me. Many things I couldn't grasp their purpose, let alone use them.

We had quite a crowd at dinner. In addition to Ronnie and his family, the Smiths, their grandparents from the trailer, joined us as well. Gloria and Mike were in Texas where they lived. The combination of food and fellowship made it the best meal I had eaten since coming to America.

More important than the food, though, were the feelings of love that the Wilsons gave me. When Mr. Wilson gave the blessing over the food, I didn't understand much of what he said except for the part where he thanked God for the food in Jesus' name. A warm feeling encompassed me. I felt genuinely welcome here. For the first time since leaving Vietnam, I felt like I was home.

Chapter 11

"Praise the LORD!
Praise God in His sanctuary;
Praise Him in His mighty expanse.
Praise Him for His mighty deeds;
Praise Him according to His excellent greatness.
Praise Him with trumpet sound;
Praise Him with harp and lyre.
Praise Him with timbrel and dancing;
Praise Him with stringed instruments and pipe.
Praise Him with loud cymbals;
Praise Him with resounding cymbals.
Let everything that has breath praise the LORD.
Praise the LORD!."

(Psalm 150:1-6)

That Sunday, I put on a dress for church. Bobbie told me that women did not wear ao dai as we did in Vietnam. She said that their church only allowed women to wear dresses, no make-up or jewelry. I didn't understand the reasoning, but I gladly complied because of the hospitality they were showering upon me.

The church service was not like anything I had ever experienced before. At home, Catholic Mass was the same every week. Women and girls sat on one side of the church and men and boys on the other. No one dared talk in the sanctuary either. The priest was the only one who spoke. If I dared to say anything, there would be consequences. I received more than a few spankings for talking in church. Nothing from that environment prepared me for a Pentecostal church service.

First, everyone sat together. That part I liked. I wouldn't have wanted to sit away from the Wilsons among all these strangers. Even before the service began, people stood up and asked prayers for people in their family or friends. A relation might be ill or undergoing surgery or maybe just taking a long trip. Whatever the reason, the congregation all agreed to pray with a resounding "Amen."

As the minister began preaching his sermon, people started shouting "Amen" or "Halleluiah" while he was talking. The sound grew in intensity as it echoed back and forth through the auditorium, with more and more people joining in the chant.

Then some people began dancing in the aisles or jumping up and down and saying crazy things that I didn't believe were English or any other language I could identify. I was shocked and more than a little frightened by the display.

I curled up in my seat, reciting the Lord's Prayer in Vietnamese over and over with my eyes looking straight down. Years ago, my father told me that there were many churches in the United States, but few people attended church. He also told me that some of the people who attended church were evil.

I only looked up one time. One lady jumped so violently that her hairpiece flew off and landed on the nearby floor. She didn't seem to notice. Goodness, she never stopped to pick it up! I had never seen anything like it before. *This was church?* I thought. Still, as unsettling as the service had been, it had been joyous, and it was obvious that the Spirit was present in the congregation. I decided that God has all kinds of followers. Who was I to judge? My mood improved even more as the joy continued after the service. Beeler took everyone out for hamburgers which as fast becoming my favorite American food.

After a week or two, I began to acclimate to my new surroundings. Beeler and Bobbie (they insisted that I called them by their first names.) arranged for me to enroll in school. I wasn't attending college; I wasn't ready for that yet. My course was an English as a Second Language class, and even I realized how much I needed that!

There were people in the class from all over the world. I was astounded by the number of languages, cultures, and countries represented in that small group – all here to learn more about our adopted country and its language.

One of the male students didn't live too far from the Wilsons. He volunteered to take me to and from school every day so that the Wilsons didn't have to drive me themselves. He was very nice and sweet, but not my type at all. I made sure to pay him a little every week to help cover the cost of his gas and never even hinted that I was interested in him.

Our teacher, Ms. Susan, was wonderful – so patient and kind. I couldn't imagine dealing with so many different cultures and languages, but she handled it with joy. She even invited the class to a swimming party at her house. I went to the party, but I didn't go swimming. The truth was that I couldn't swim. Dodging bullets and bombs and doing housework hadn't left much time for things like that. I also didn't feel comfortable in my swimming suit that Bobbie had bought me. Even though I knew these people, my self-confidence was lacking.

So, I remained by the side of the pool and

helped Ms. Susan with the cooking chores, which was something that I could do well. Over the past weeks, Bobbie had instructed me to use many of the common utensils in American kitchens.

While Ms. Susan and I cooked the hamburgers, we laughed and joked with those in the pool and the hijinks they were doing. Being a part of a group, especially a group of people I now called friends, was special, a different kind of special than a family special. I had never experienced anything like this before.

Three months had passed since I came to California to be with the Wilsons. They treated me like I was their daughter, and I loved the feelings of love that surrounded me. I no longer jumped when someone screamed at church or spoke in tongues though I never felt the urge to do either myself.

As I got to know more and more people in the church community, I realized that they were good people trying, as I was, to be good Christians. Being a practicing Christian meant one had to practice. The church often had revivals, each bringing in a visiting preacher to lead it. More often than not, the Wilsons would invite that pastor over for dinner one night during his stay.

Beeler encouraged me to be friendly with these men when they came over. He told me more than once that I should smile more and frown less to make them feel welcome. Sometimes, I wondered if he wanted me to date them. I realized that Beeler only wanted me to be happy. His daughter had found happiness with a pastor and was living a full life – he wanted the same for me.

I tried to oblige, but I just couldn't find a way to patch the hole in my heart. I couldn't allow myself to move forward in my life. As much as I tried to forget Shady, his shadow was always hanging over me. Because of him, I was still very much alone even among all this love.

One time, a young evangelist came to speak at our church. Sister Brown, who sat two rows in front of me, stood up and said, "Please pray for my son. He is dating a Catholic girl, and I fear for his soul since she is going to hell." I felt like a brick had hit me. After all, I am a Catholic girl. Am I going to hell? Why?

I looked to the preacher to hear what he had to say but was not ready when he said, "I know what you mean. When I went to a Catholic church to meet with the priest there, he gave me a can of beer and a cigar!" I was confused. I had not been to a Catholic church here in America. From what the pastor said, I imagined that people solely went to the Catholic church to drink beer and smoke cigars. I had a hard time even imagining it! I tried to picture the church buildings with smoke pouring out of the windows and beer cans on the sidewalk.

After we got home, I discussed what the pastor said with Beeler and Bobbie. I explained that; however Catholics acted here in America, Catholic worship had been nothing like that in Vietnam. They didn't say anything; they just looked uncomfortable. I guess they didn't know either.

I could see that even talking about the subject seemed to upset them, so I let it drop and never mentioned it again. The Wilsons had been so kind to me, opening their home and practically adopting me that I didn't want to hurt them. I did, however, pay closer attention whenever we passed a church. I figured I could tell which one was Catholic by the smoke rising from the roof.

After two weeks, I passed by many churches, and I still hadn't found any smoking ones. I did get up the courage to ask Ms. Susan whether Catholics in America were how the pastor had described them. She told me that she was a Catholic and that beer and cigars were not how services were here. She also told me that she would be happy to take me to Mass and prove it to me. I thanked her and politely refused her offer. I didn't want to upset the Wilsons any more than I had.

After that week, I'd set two goals for when I got my driver's license. The first was to find a Catholic church and see for myself what went on inside. The second was to find a Coke machine. I had first heard about the magical Coke machines from one of my high school teachers. He had been to the United States over one of our breaks and brought many stories back.

The way he talked about the Coke machine, I envisioned it to be a small room where ghosts would take your money when you pushed a button. Other spirits would bring you your Coke and your change. I had to see one of these machines for myself.

Chapter 12

*"The Lord is not slow about His promise, as some count
slowness, but is patient toward you, not wishing for any to
perish but for all to come to repentance."*

(2 Peter 3:9)

One reason I couldn't let go of Shady was that he couldn't let go of me. It wasn't that I thought about him all the time. He called me every week without fail. This behavior toyed with my feelings to the point that I felt I was being torn apart. I came close to refusing to speak to him at all, but I couldn't do that. I loved hearing his voice on the phone. Despite the pain, I lived for his calls.

So, every week I would pretend to be brave and ask him about his week, his wife, and the children. My heart burned as I spoke the words and heard his response. I never once hinted that he should pursue a divorce. That was not my decision to make. Every time we spoke, I felt a nail pierce my heart. At the end of the call, I would beat myself up for not having the courage to put an end to whatever this was.

I did try to get on with my life. A man in my class, Victor, was very nice. He was from Mexico, where he was an engineer. We would laugh and joke all the time. He had been sent to the United States to learn English. He even taught me some Spanish, *te quiero mucho*. He told me that it meant he liked me. I didn't trust him, so I asked Ms. Susan, who told me that it meant he loved me very much.

Victor asked me out, but I wasn't sure what to do. I asked Bobbie, who told me that I shouldn't until he went to church with us. I wasn't sure that was the answer, but I realized that I wasn't ready for another romance either, so I turned down his offer – gently, I hoped. Here again, Shady's shadow was upon me. I had known Shady for years, yet he had betrayed me. How could I trust someone I had only known for a few months?

Nonetheless, my flirtations with Victor had reminded me of someone else in my past that I had cared for, Michael. He currently lived in North Carolina and had given me his address before he had shipped out of Vietnam. On a whim, I sent him a letter.

Imagine my surprise when he sent me a letter only a week later. He told me that he remembered me and missed me. He was currently going to university, studying to become a lawyer. I wrote him back and impulsively sent the Wilson's phone number, never really expecting a call.

He called! I couldn't believe it when I heard his voice on the line. He was excited that I was in the United States and was planning to stay here. He wondered if it would be okay for him to come to California for a visit when he had a break from school during the summer. I panicked. Things were happening way too fast. What should I say? I wasn't sure, my heart was in turmoil, but my brain stepped up and said, "Yes!"

Only two weeks later, I got an unexpected call

from Shady. His wife had filed for divorce, and he was cooperating so that the process could move forward quickly. He also told me that he had taken a job in Vietnam, and he needed to leave soon.

He was so sorry for how he had treated me and begged my forgiveness. Then he dropped the bombshell. He wanted nothing more in the world than for me to accompany him back to Saigon as his wife as soon as the divorce was final.

Now I was really confused. Here was a man that I had moved halfway around the world to marry – a man who then betrayed my love – a man who had caused me more grief and tears than anything in my young life, and he wants me to marry him? Yet, in my heart, I still loved him. Forgiveness would take some time, but my love had never faded. I said, "Yes."

Two weeks later, Shady came to Bakersfield to see me. I was excited to see him, of course, but the vision of his wife standing by his side at the airport in Atlanta still haunted me – still hurt me. We talked and talked. Slowly, as the weekend progressed, forgiveness seemed more plausible than it had before. I knew there would be no way I could forget what had happened between us, but I could forgive him for it. We could move on with our lives – together.

I told him about my correspondence with Michael. We called him at once and explained what had happened – how Shady and I had found each other again. I told Michael that I still cared for him, but I loved Shady more. He told me that he was disappointed, but he understood. He congratulated Shady and me on our engagement. I hoped that I had not hurt him too badly. That conversation was the last time he and I ever spoke.

Shady and I spent the next two days getting reacquainted. He took me downtown to a nice restaurant, where we continued talking about the changes in our lives and the big change we were about to take. At night, Shady stayed in the room with the Wilsons' boys. He and I had reconciled, but we weren't married yet.

When we took Shady to the airport, en route to Saigon, he and I had another tearful goodbye. I gave him a note asking my father to rent a room to Shady for Shady's safety while in Vietnam. I also told Father that I was currently living in California, where I could go to school for free, and planned to spend Christmas with Phan in Phoenix. I didn't mention anything about Shady marrying his ex-wife again or his pending divorce. Some things needed to be kept secret, at least for now.

During Christmas break, I went to see Phan as I had told my father I would. I wanted to save money, so I took the bus. Wow! What a long bus ride! I couldn't wait to see Phan and eat some real Vietnamese cooking again. Don't get me wrong, Bobbie was a fantastic chef, but my palate longed for a taste of home. My sister didn't let me down. That night we had the best sweet and sour soup with pork. I can still taste it.

Phan and I talked about everything. I told her about Shady and what was happening in our lives. She loved me and promised not to say a word until I was ready. The two weeks in Phoenix flew by. Why is it that joyous times always go by so fast? I took the bus back to Bakersfield and the Wilsons, who welcomed me again with open arms like a daughter who had left and returned to them.

My "adopted" family was truly amazing. I loved all of them as much as I loved my own family back home. In addition to my schoolwork, I tried more and more to help where I could. I joined the young adult group at the church and even went with them to Disneyland, an incredible adventure. I think it would take a separate book to document just that trip.

On April 20th, Bobbie gave me something I had never experienced before – a birthday party. What fun! I invited a lot of my friends, mostly from the church. Bobbie had doubts about some of my other friends, so I left them off my list. We never discussed church, so I wasn't sure where my school friends went or even if they went to church at all. Not going to church would be a deal-breaker for Bobbie.

Only six months later, I received the long-awaited news. Shady's divorce was final. He wrote me to let me know. He told me that he would be in Phoenix in a few weeks and wanted to marry me while he was there. If I left California right away, I could arrange for a church and a minister to perform the ceremony.

My "sister," Gloria, told me right away that she would make my dress for me. She was a fantastic seamstress who made much of her clothing. I was delighted to have her make mine.

Bobbie gave me a wedding shower at the house attended by some of my friends from the church. Of course, I told my classmates that I was leaving to be married. I felt awful knowing that we would probably never meet again. I would miss them all terribly.

I knew then that God had sent these people to me. They were angels sent to help me through the most trying part of my life so far. I don't think I would have made it without them. Although Bobbie and Beeler passed away years ago, Gloria and I still stay in touch. Their memory will be with me always.

Chapter 13

"Love is patient, love is kind and is not jealous; love does not brag and is not arrogant does not act unbecomingly; it does not seek its own, is not provoked, does not take into account a wrong suffered..."

(1 Corinthians 13:4-5)

The bus ride from Bakersfield to Phoenix was no shorter than before, but I filled that time with thoughts of Shady coming back from Vietnam and our upcoming wedding, so the trip seemed to take no time at all. On the way, I even got one of my questions answered – the magical Coke machine. Much to my disappointment, it wasn't magic at all. There were no ghosts either. I put my dollar into the slot, the device recognized it, gave me a Coke, and my change in return. Tasty but disappointing all the same.

Phan picked me up from the bus station in Phoenix and made me my favorite Vietnamese dinner – sweet and sour soup as a welcoming gift. The very next day, I started going through a list of churches trying to find someone who would marry Shady and me.

The Catholic church refused to marry us because Shady had been married before and was not Catholic. Without an annulment, they wouldn't consider it, and we had no time to complete all the paperwork for that.

Other churches had different reasons but the same answer – not here. Finally, almost in despair and at the end of my list, I found a wedding chapel that would accommodate us.

Shady arrived from Vietnam the next day, and he and I got caught up in a whirlwind of activity.

There were so many things to do. First, we had to get a blood test and then take the results to the courthouse to get our marriage license. From there, we went to the chapel, where the staff had arranged for a minister to do the ceremony.

Our wedding took place on October 16, 1973. It was a small affair. No one from Bakersfield could come, so my sister and her husband and some of her friends were the only people there. Shady and I didn't care. We lost ourselves in each other's eyes. Marrying him was all I had ever wanted. The size of the wedding didn't matter at all.

After the wedding, we took a few days to get all our paperwork ironed out, not much of a honeymoon. We had to go to the Federal Court House to get my passport altered to reflect my name change. That part was easy, but there seemed to be an endless number of forms to complete and minor obstacles to overcome as well.

All that didn't matter. I was with Shady and would be returning with him to my home in Vietnam. I had only been gone for a year, yet a burning inside of me longed to return home. I had to wonder, though, what kind of reception the two of us would receive.

I shouldn't have worried. Father was delighted to see me, as were my sisters and brother. They seemed overjoyed to see me. Shady and I begged

Father's forgiveness for the way we had gotten married and the deceptions we had played on him along our path. I had never thought of my father as a forgiving person, but he found the grace to forgive us somehow. He told us that we might be married in the United States, but now we had to have a Vietnamese wedding party.

The next morning Shady and I worked on the wedding announcements which Father sent a few days later to our friends and relatives. even some of them who still lived in our old village of Tu Chau in North Vietnam. Several aunts and uncles came over to the house to discuss the details of the reception. We decided on a small affair, only ten tables, and invited our closest friends and relatives.

According to Vietnamese tradition, we prepare a small bag containing tea, betel leaves, areca nuts, and cookies to deliver along with the wedding invitations. Shady was curious as to the contents of the package. Tea and cookies made sense, but why betel and areca?

Although consumed by many Asians, these items created a mild high and were considered potentially harmful. I explained to him that this was tradition – traditions that had spanned over one-thousand years of our history. Another part of that tradition meant that he and I had to hand-deliver the bags to the invited people. Of course, he didn't accept the explanation without further explanation. I don't think he would have believed me otherwise.

The legend was that a pair of twin brothers fell in love with the same woman. She was beautiful and the subject of much admiration in the village. Tan, who was a few minutes older than his brother, called upon the tradition that the eldest should marry first and claimed his bride, leaving his brother, Lang, to mourn his loss.

Several months later, Lang came home for a visit. He and his brother looked so much alike that his sister-in-law mistook him for her husband and took him to her bed. Lang, still smitten by her, did not refuse.

Later, when the deception became known, Lang felt tremendous remorse for the lewd act he had inflicted on his brother and sister-in-law. In shame, he fled far away to a distant river, where he died. A tall, slender tree grew on that spot, which bore nuts as its fruit.

Despite what had happened, Tan missed his brother and went off searching for Lang. By chance, his wanderings led him to the same spot where his brother had died. Leaning against the areca nut tree that had sprung from Lang, he died and transformed into a block of limestone.

Now, Tan's wife was so distraught when he did not return that she also set out in search. After a time, she also chanced upon where the two brothers had died. She was so tired and hungry that she sat on the limestone and cried for her lost husband. She also collapsed and died. She became the betel vine that crept and twined around the limestone block.

The story finished, Shady and I sat quietly for a moment. He gently took my hand, looked into my eyes, and said, "I will never leave you again. I will always be faithful to you and promise to love you until the day I die." I smiled and assured him that I felt the same way.

Shady and I remained in Vietnam for the next eight months when, in 1974, the United States government decided that they needed him back home. This time, though, they were sending him to Tinker Air Force Base in Oklahoma instead of Georgia. I found it extremely painful to leave my family for a second time. Being gone for a year had given me a new appreciation for my family. Oklahoma was an unknown for Shady and me both. We had no idea what Oklahoma would be like, but we prayed that God would continue to walk with us there.

Chapter 14

*"There is neither * Jew nor Greek, there is neither * slave nor free man, there is neither male nor female; for you are all one in Christ Jesus."*

(Galatians 3:28)

I have never understood how people could judge a person simply by their appearance. The outer shell of clothing and color did not reflect the person's true self any more than the peel on a piece of fruit accurately predicts the state of the edible part inside.

Shady and I had put up with a lot of racism in Vietnam. Stares from passersby, casual comments told in a quiet voice just loud enough for me to hear, and actual shouts of racial slurs from others. Of course, all of that was aimed at Shady and me through association.

We found things to be a little better in Oklahoma. One reason was we were poor. We didn't have any money, so there was no temptation to go out to eat or a movie. Much of Shady's pay went to his ex-wife and children in the form of alimony and child support. What was left was all we had until his next payday.

Out of necessity, the only people we associated with were either people from the church or work friends of Shady. I had met several Vietnamese women through a Mary Kay salesperson shortly after we arrived. They all had married Americans, which gave us a lot in common. We would get together every weekend to gossip and talk about our lives.

Because of Shady and my limited outside exposure, racism didn't play a big part in our everyday lives. Financially, however, we struggled.

Every month was a challenge to stretch what Shady made to the next payday. The payments to his ex-wife were taking their toll. Shady did his best to provide for us. Things finally improved when Shady managed to get a part-time job that supplemented his government salary.

Life was not so simple whenever we ventured out of our "bubble" into the world outside. Shady's children still lived near Atlanta. Distance and cost meant that he didn't get to see them often. There was one time we went to Georgia expressly to visit his children. I remember going to the mall in Atlanta where strangers openly pointed at us, and passersby threw hateful comments at us. It was just like back in Vietnam in reverse. This time the slurs were directed at me. That day "gook" became part of my vocabulary. I hated it.

Shady's sister and the rest of his family still lived in Alabama. Whenever we were visiting his children, we would also try to stop and see them. Although his family accepted me with open arms, other people's reaction to me was even worse than those people in Atlanta.

Part of me always thought that Shady would have liked to live near his sister, but he realized that would be impossible with a Vietnamese wife. He was always pensive whenever we visited his family. He told me that I must never go anywhere alone, even during the daytime. I shouldn't be out at all at night, even with others. I felt like a prisoner in my sister-in-law's house.

Even though life wasn't easy at times, it was our life now – his and mine together. I cherished my husband and longed to do my part to support our life together. Unfortunately, without an education, my efforts were severely limited.

To start that process, I enrolled at Rose State College in 1974. It was within walking distance of our home in Midwest City, Oklahoma, and seemed a good place to start. I was still unable to drive, and with his two jobs, Shady could not take me back and forth during the day. I would have to stay at the college. I considered that more time to study, and Shady supported and encouraged me even when I became discouraged with my progress.

I found the first semester to be the hardest. I enrolled in only three classes – English Composition I, Conversational French, and Political Science. In my mind, I thought I was starting slow. French class was a breeze since I had studied it in high school, and my father often spoke it around the house. However, the other two classes gave me more than a few problems.

English Comp was a contract class. We made a deal with the teacher based on what grade we wanted to receive. I wanted an A. The contract said that I had to submit a five-page paper at the end of the course to qualify and do well on the mid-term and final exams. I faithfully attended classes, did well on the tests – though not as well as I had hoped, and submitted the paper. All my work wasn't quite up to an A. I got a B instead. Still, not bad for someone who learned English as a third language!

Political Science was the worst. I have never worked so hard in a class. I didn't understand anything my teacher said. Apparently, unknown to me, political vocabulary wasn't a part of the normal spoken English. I had to use a dictionary to look up almost every word! Fortunately, I had lots of time to spend studying in the library, and I used that time well, taking only a small bit of time to eat the lunch I had packed.

In the mid-70s, Vietnam was a controversial subject. Consequently, we talked about Vietnam quite a bit in that class. I tried to shrink down in my seat as all eyes focused on me during those discussions. Most of my classmates said terrible things about my home country that I didn't understand. The boys, in particular, were brutal in their language.

Some of them claimed that Vietnam was hell, and they were so glad that they never had to go there. I didn't understand how they could condemn someplace they did not know, but they did.

A woman ranted about her son being a soldier in Vietnam and related some of his experiences. I cornered her after class to talk to her about him. She seemed nervous and refused to look me in the eye. She told me that her son wouldn't want to talk to me. This comment confused me. I hadn't asked to speak with him. Before saying goodbye, I thanked her for her son's service to my country.

Regardless of my efforts, I didn't pass the first test in Political Science. I was beside myself. I had done poorly on exams before but had never failed. My professor took pity on me and allowed me to retake the test in her office, where I could have more time and not be under the scrutiny of my classmates. She allowed me to do the same thing for the final. I was so thankful. I wouldn't have made my way through the class otherwise. At the end of the term, I wore my grade of C like a badge of honor.

My goal when I started college was to go to dental school. Dentistry had been a dream since my youth. When I was little, we didn't have money to go to the dentist, so we had to go to the free dental clinic instead.

The problem with the clinic was that you had to get a number for an appointment. Sometimes, I would wait the entire day for them to call my number. Other times, the clinic would close before my turn, which meant I had to return the following day and repeat the entire process. This experience made me want to be a dentist. I wanted to return to Vietnam someday and help poor people who needed care.

With my becoming more involved outside the home, my inability to drive became a real problem. Shady had to take me wherever I wanted to go, and having a second driver would help immensely.

From the onset of my driver training, I was scared to death. The car was so big, and I was so small. The other cars were going so fast! Shady made a bad situation worse with his teaching style. He lacked patience. We had more than a few screaming sessions during my lessons with him. Fortunately for our marriage, a friend's daughter-in-law offered to teach me. Shady quickly agreed, and I was extremely grateful. She was a teacher by profession and was very patient with me. After only a few weeks, I passed my test!

As Shady and I grew into our marriage, the world around us ceased to be as important. I still received letters from home and responded as soon as possible, but those took weeks to exchange. The news wasn't news by the time it reached either place. That all changed on April 30, 1975.

Chapter 15

"He said,
'What do you see, Amos?' And I said,
'A basket of summer fruit.'
Then the LORD said to me,
'The end has come for My people Israel.
I will spare them no longer"

(Amos 5:2)

How does one deal with sudden change, especially one that changes their lives and their family's lives forever? Yesterday, there was a South Vietnam; today, there wasn't. In history, the collapse of the South on April 30, 1975, would hardly be a blip on a timeline, but for the people involved, the defeat wore heavily. As Saigon fell, the country collapsed like a string of dominoes as the North Vietnamese invaders passed through without incident.

Since the peace accord in 1972, there had been indications that such a thing might happen, but those were subjects discussed over tea in a Saigon restaurant – not in the American living rooms. Since the withdrawal of American troops, American media didn't talk about Vietnam very often, if at all. South Vietnam wasn't news in America until it disappeared entirely.

I distinctly remember staring at the television news in disbelief as thousands of my countrymen converged on the U.S. Embassy in Saigon. I watched transfixed as thousands more loaded up ships, recently from the South Vietnamese navy, attempting to leave the country. The crowds packed the airport, frantic to get a flight to anywhere other than here. The people stayed there even after the North Vietnamese began shelling the tarmac, effectively closing off any chance of escape by air.

As more and more avenues of escape closed, thousands more attempted to find refuge in anything that would float in the hope that the small boat would make it to the U.S. Navy vessels located somewhere off the coast. The escape boats had no directional equipment and were woefully overcrowded. The occupants relied solely on luck and sheer will. The country I still loved was in chaos, and tears streamed from my face in the realization that there was nothing I could do.

Of course, my first thoughts were about my family living in Bien Hoa. How were they? What were they going through? I had scanned through the crowds on the news looking for a familiar face, but there had not been one. The news reports spoke of street fighting in Saigon as Viet Cong went house to house looking for South Vietnamese officials and American sympathizers.

My heart went into my throat. My father was a South Vietnamese police lieutenant and head of Internal Security in Bien Hoa, and my stepmother had worked with the Americans at their army base. What would become of them? Were they even still alive? If the Viet Cong had taken our parents, what would happen to my sisters and brother? I was helpless. There was no one I could ask. Officially, Vietnam was closed off to the world.

My patience grew thin while waiting on word

about my family. Being helpless was not something I handled well. I needed to do something to help my countrymen, if not my family. That something came in the form of thousands of Vietnamese and Cambodian refugees flooding into America. They came with nothing but the clothing on their backs and maybe some now worthless Vietnamese money. Anyone who spoke Vietnamese and English was suddenly in great demand. I found a purpose. I became a translator.

The work was steady, but like all bureaucratic work, it began slowly as the government struggled to adapt to this new reality. Because of Shady's prior experience with the Department of Defense in Vietnam, the commanding general at Tinker Air Force Base contacted him to enlist our help.

Several South Vietnamese military leaders and their families had escaped during the last days and were already at Tinker. All of them, especially the women and children, were frightened and confused. The Air Force needed our assistance to help them assimilate into American society.

Shady and I both had responsibilities in this endeavor. I worked closely with the families, primarily as a teaching assistant. I don't believe I ever knew what Shady was doing during this time. I was far too busy with my part of the deal.

All the problems I had encountered on my

arrival flooded back to me as I worked with these mothers and their children. Part of that job was trying to teach them English, of course, but an even greater task was helping them adjust to the alienness of their new environment. I knew that very little of their Vietnamese cultural background would translate to the United States. Slowly we waded through everything they needed to know to survive here.

When the time finally came to introduce the children to the Midwest City/Del City Schools, I accompanied them to their classroom as a translator. I felt so badly for these women and children. I had asked for this transition to America – begged for it; they had not. They had been perfectly happy with their lives in South Vietnam. There, they had been privileged society ladies. They had never counted on these changes to their circumstances.

I volunteered to work with all the refugee students in the Mid-Del school district during the summer of 1975. I loved the work, and I felt useful working with them. At this time, I still had not heard anything about my family, and this was a way that I felt useful.

The personal satisfaction I felt helping young people succeed in their new language and country was incredible. That was when I gave up on my dream of dentistry and decided to become a teacher instead. I finished my associate's degree at Rose State and then continued my education at Central State University, now known as the University of Central Oklahoma.

All did not go smoothly on my path. As part of the teacher education program, the school required me to observe a teacher in the classroom for several days during the semester. I made the arrangements with a local school and watched the teacher at work. On my last day of observation, she pulled me aside. She told me that my accent was too strong, that the students could never understand me. She suggested that I change my major away from education.

Her review crushed me. I had received many compliments from students and teachers alike while tutoring Algebra at Rose State. I enjoyed working with young people, helping them succeed, especially when race or language had tied their hands. The students I had tutored seemed to do well. I could not imagine a future without being a teacher.

I dried my tears. One teacher was not going to change my mind. If the students I had worked with believed in me, then I could believe in myself. I stood my ground, kept my major, and received my degree. I was a teacher!

Chapter 16

"Train up a child in the way he should go,
Even when he is old he will not depart from it."

(Proverbs 22:6)

While I was working with the local Vietnamese refugees, I finally heard back from my sister, Vinh, in Vietnam. She could not send the letter directly to me. Instead, she used the nephew of a friend, Nga Fish, who lived in Paris. The word I received was not good. As I had suspected, the Viet Cong had arrested my father almost immediately after Saigon's fall, taking him to a reeducation camp somewhere in the north. My stepmother, frantic to feed her children, bought dried fish in another town and brought it back to Bien Hoa, where she tried to sell it at a local market near the house.

Her prospects were not good. She didn't know anyone at the market, and they mistreated her, partly because she was competition but mostly because they feared the Communists. Father's "sins" apparently stained the entire family. It was like a dark cloud followed them everywhere they went. Not to be discouraged, my stepmother continued her work at the market, gradually gathering the respect of the other vendors and customers. The family barely survived.

This news was terrible. Although greatly saddened by the state of my family, I also realized that there was nothing I could do about it here in Oklahoma. They were more than half a world away, thoroughly shut off from me by the Communist regime and by the ongoing war of words between our two governments. We were unable to send letters directly until 1980 when the political landscape settled down. Until that time, routing letters through Paris had to suffice. We would send letters to him, and he would forward them to Vietnam or the U.S. He was our lifeline.

According to my sister Vinh's letter, one of their biggest challenges came when the Communists changed the currency. Overnight, the old South Vietnamese dong was worthless. Only the new money was valid. All people could do was trade their old currency for new at a government exchange point.

Typical of the Communists, the government didn't do an equal exchange either. The old money traded at five hundred to one. After exchanging their money, many people didn't have enough currency to buy food for their families. Some of the wealthier families found a way to game the system by having poor people exchange cash for a piece of the proceeds.

Through the turmoil of reunification, the government tried to subsidize the population through commissary allotments. Officials would give each family a ticket indicating how much rice, milk, meat, and other food the government rationed. My stepmother soon found a way to make a profit from this procedure.

It was frighteningly simple. Some people didn't need the government supplies. They preferred to have the cash to buy what they needed on the black market. My stepmother would buy their tickets from them for much less than they were worth. She then turned around and sold those same tickets to others at a slightly higher rate. The money she made wasn't a lot, but it did allow the family to keep going.

One of the greatest fears was that the government would take the house from them. The government had already taken several homes in our area to provide housing for new North Vietnamese families moving south to take administrative jobs in the government. The family wondered when the day would come when they wanted our home.

My sister, Hanh, applied to work for the government in the communications office. The communication committee tasked her group with "selling" the new government to the people through music.

Hanh was an accomplished singer and got the job easily. She traveled around the country singing the praises of the new regime, even though she didn't believe half of what she was singing. With her loyalty proven, the authorities allowed her to get a job at a movie theater. Since the only people who could now afford movies were high in the government, she used that opportunity to make influential friends and, through them, save the house from confiscation.

Later, Hanh and one of her singing friends got together on a retail enterprise. The friend had connections within the open market, also known as the black market in Bien Hoa. Consequently, she could purchase things not readily available to the public – cigarettes in particular, although they also had books, pencils, and condensed milk. These were very high-demand items and increasingly hard to find. She and Hanh started a daily run from Bien Hoa to Ho Chi Minh City, the old Saigon, to resell these items. Their venture proved very profitable.

My sister, Vinh, graduated from high school in 1975 – third in her class. Her accomplishment should have been a joyous time for her, except for her parentage. The authorities denied her entrance into every college for no other reason than my father had worked for the enemy and her Catholic religion.

Undeterred, she took a test for entry into medical school, thinking that path would provide her with a means to succeed. She studied diligently alongside the daughter of a high-ranking official. Both girls studied hard and knew the same answers. In the end, Vinh had failed, but her friend had passed.

My brother, He, worked diligently in the community, volunteering for every possible assignment. Soon, he had earned the respect of the local party officials and was designated to represent our family at neighborhood meetings. These meetings were not optional – someone from the family had to attend. He told my stepmother and sisters that the meeting was nothing more than an opportunity for the government to solicit information about neighbors who might be hoarding supplies and wealth.

The same attitude took place in the schools. Teachers would ask students what they ate at home and what their family did to earn a living. Then they would tell their pupils that the government cared for them more than their parents did. When students provided information about their parents, they received rewards and praise.

Most of my siblings were savvy enough to see through the government's ruse, but they had to be very careful what they said and did around Lan. She was my daughter. Shady and I had adopted her as a baby while we were in Vietnam, but she was too young to go back to the United States with us. Then the Communists came, and she couldn't leave. She was young and impressionable and liked her Communist teachers far too much. Things were getting scarier over there. I prayed that we could find a solution soon.

The answer to my prayers was the Orderly

Departure Program. The ODP was a product of the United Nations High Commissioner for Refugees (UNHCR), and the United States was a participant. The world had stood in horror while tens of thousands of Vietnamese and Chinese-Vietnamese persons perished in the South China Sea. Estimates indicated that over 500,000 had died in the South China Sea either by drowning or piracy. This program was the world's solution.

As soon as I could apply, I began the process of getting my family into the U.S. The application wasn't easy. Not only was there a lot of paperwork to complete, but there was also the matter of dealing with the Vietnamese government. Again, the "treasonous" acts of my father hampered my efforts. The Communist officials saw the ODP as an opportunity to exact vengeance on the rest of them. The process was hard on most people but proved nearly impossible for them.

To the Communist Vietnamese government, my father was a war criminal. His service to the South Vietnamese Police had guaranteed prison time for him after reunification. The conditions in these "reeducation" facilities were horrendous. He was given only a small bowl of plain rice every day. After more than three years and in poor health, the government sent him back to our family to live out the rest of his life.

Lan opened the door when he arrived. He was so emaciated that she didn't recognize him. She was certain that he was one of the many street beggars looking for food. She slammed the door in his face.

My father knocked again. This time he announced, "Lan, I am your grandfather. Open the door!" This time she looked closer at the withered man at the door and realized who it was. She told me that she almost knocked him over with her welcome.

Later he recounted what the Viet Cong had done to him. Because of his involvement with the former government, the Viet Cong had ordered him to report for reeducation allowing only two changes of clothes and ten days' food to accompany him. He and the other detainees were immediately put into closed vehicles without windows and taken to a camp somewhere in the country.

The camp was large and hosted about five hundred prisoners. Here they were tortured, starved, and worked in the fields and jungle. They were also forced to write confessions for the "crimes" they had committed. The confession had to go back for three generations – to the sins of fathers and grandfathers. The papers Father wrote admitted he had done wrong, that he had sold out his country and committed an act of treason by helping the Americans. He said further that what he did was out of ignorance and stupidity.

Failure to write a perfect confession resulted in torture. Beatings were common as was isolation in enclosed rooms barely large enough for one person where the prisoner was chained so that even limited movement was impossible.

His captors gave him a cup of rice and some vegetables in the morning. Hunger was ever present in the camp. One prisoner was tending the camp garden and was shot for taking a potato for himself. My father was fortunate in that he had jungle labor. He and the others found leaves, crickets, and sometimes snakes that they could eat to supplement their diet.

Many prisoners died of starvation, dysentery, malaria, beriberi, or tuberculosis. Their mass graves created the perimeter of the camp and served as a reminder for what awaited many others before their time was over.

His last year of imprisonment, he was assigned as a medical assistant to a doctor in the north who took pity on dad. After their time was done, the doctor arranged for father's release because of his health.

The stigma of his past continued even after he had returned home and regained some of his strength. His association with the South Vietnamese government assured him that no one would dare hire him. He was limited to working in the market with his wife and children.

One would have thought that the government would have been glad to be done with him – not so. The government wanted still more – this time from me. For every piece of paper I sent to Vietnam, the Vietnamese government required a special "fee."

Even though Shady and I were barely getting by as it was, I found ways to come up with the money to pay the bribes – almost $20,000 so far. There was no choice. I had to gain my family's release.

In 1982, I finally received some good news about my family. The Red Cross telephoned and told me that my brother, He, had escaped Vietnam and was in a refugee camp on Bi Dong Island in Malaysia. I was so happy. Finally, a light in the darkness to give us hope. Since I had already filed the paperwork for sponsorship, he only had to stay on the island for two weeks before coming to Oklahoma.

When He arrived, he had quite a story to share. The voyage on the boat had been plagued by storms and pirates who took everything they had and left them adrift on the sea. The Christians on board prayed for deliverance from what appeared to be certain death. Just as they were about to give up, they saw a little island on the horizon. At first, they thought they were back in Vietnam, but after landing, were overjoyed to discover they were in

Malaysia instead. The castaways stayed with the natives on the island, enjoying their hospitality, until the coast guard arrived to take them to Bi Dong.

Heartened by He's release, I renewed the struggle to get the rest of the family out of Vietnam. Finally, almost four years after I began the process, my family arrived in Oklahoma. They stayed with Shady and me until they could get by independently. For some of them, that time was almost ten years. I didn't care. We were a family again.

Chapter 17

"The LORD is the one who goes ahead of you; He will be with you. He will not fail you or forsake you. Do not fear or be dismayed."

(Deuteronomy 31:8)

After graduating from teacher's college, I found that the next step would be even more challenging – finding an actual teaching job. However, nothing prepared me for the anti-Asian sentiment within the professional education environment. Since coming to the United States, I had been the object of bigotry several times. One look at me was all they needed to reject me out of hand.

I had first encountered this bias during my student observations two years earlier, but, in my naivete, I had assumed that the teacher involved was an isolated incident. That was not the case. During my student teaching, my assigned teacher and principal were very impressed with my abilities and had written glowing recommendations. My principal had gone as far as to contact another principal in the Mid-Del district regarding a third-grade position that he had. The man seemed agreeable to meeting me, so my principal encouraged me to apply.

The interview was cordial. In my mind, it had gone exceedingly well. All indications were that I had the job – until I didn't. Of course, I was disappointed, but that didn't stop me from applying for other openings. In each case, the administrator refused to hire me. After suffering several rejections, I inadvertently discovered that the issue was not my ability; it was my ethnicity. I was Asian, not black or white. Administrators were sensitive to their black and white ratios. Although the Civil Right Act of 1964 prohibited discrimination based on race, color, or national origin in any program or activity that received Federal funds, to them the laws were in place to guarantee a certain balance between the two primary groups. There were no such concerns for Asians. People seemed to feel that we were more suited to mathematics and science, but they didn't think of us in education.

This revelation discouraged and depressed me. How was I to succeed if I couldn't even get a position? In my despair, I did what I always did – I prayed. I begged God to show me how best to serve his people. If I wasn't to be a teacher, what should I do?

I never expected a miracle, but my God answered my prayers in less than a week. I received a call from Oklahoma City Public Schools. The human resources person there asked if I could please come in for an interview the next day. Despite the other rejections, I was encouraged that they had contacted me. Of course, I could!

During the interview process, the administrator told me that he was looking for an Asian-American to teach at his school, Polk Fifth Year Center. He explained that many refugees relocated to the district after the fall of Saigon. Many of them were in the area his school serviced. He needed someone just like me, and he offered me the job on the spot. I couldn't believe it; I had a teaching job! Better yet, he needed me to start right away. I was to report the following Monday.

I contacted the principal the next day and asked if I could come see my classroom. I couldn't wait to get started. I wanted to get things ready for Monday – decorate the bulletin boards and arrange the seats. There was so much to do in preparation. I took home all the texts I would use to prepare myself for the week ahead.

An old doubt filtered through my mind in the middle of all the excitement – my accent. Even after spending so many years here and studying English diligently, my accent was very strong and pronounced. What if the children weren't able to understand me? What if the parents became upset at having an Asian teacher for their child? I pushed those thoughts away. God had opened this door for me, and I knew that he would not allow me to fail.

The next three years at Polk were wonderful. I had mostly LEP (Limited English Proficiency) students, which was okay by me. My language shortcomings were not a problem here. I actually believed that they helped me. The children seemed to identify with my appearance and accent. I was more like them. The children and I both grew together.

One place where my class fell behind the other

classrooms was in intermural competitions. My Asian students were so much smaller than their American counterparts that intermural sports activities were difficult. My other students, especially my American students, hated losing every time. I told them that so long as they tried their best in every competition – and I was watching to be sure they did – I would reward them with Coke and popcorn and allow them to play their math games. After a while, they didn't seem to mind losing, so long as they had tried their best.

Oklahoma weather was particularly concerning for my Asian students. They were no strangers to rain, but thunderstorms were something else entirely. When storms happened during the day, I would turn off the lights and gather my students around me on the floor in a corner of the room. Then, I told them a scary story, never telling them the ending. Their job was to tell the story's conclusion for their creative writing assignment. After a while, the children were no longer fearful of the storms. Some of them even began looking forward to them.

Although I could only speak Vietnamese, my principal assumed that I could communicate with all our Asian students because of my appearance. Each time an Asian student came to enroll – Vietnamese, Laotian, Cambodian, Thai, Chinese, he came to me. He would summon me to help. I repeatedly reminded him that this student was a Laotian or a Cambodian. The next one might be Chinese, Hmong, or Japanese. His response was always the same, "Mrs. Anderson, you can do it." Then I would call upon all my talents to communicate with the child and parent. I used my hands as well as my facial expressions to help them. I don't believe that my principal ever thought for a moment that I had the same communication problems with those students as he did.

I loved all my students equally; I didn't want my American students to feel that I treated the Asian students any better than I treated them because I was Vietnamese. If one of my Vietnamese students spoke to me in Vietnamese, I always answered them in English. I also understood how students this age think. I made a rule not to allow any Asian students to teach American students any phrases that were not appropriate for the classroom – and vice-versa. They thought it was funny that I even knew those words.

In 1981, I took a job as Bilingual Resource Teacher at Edgemere Elementary School. The Oklahoma City Public School District had received the first Federal Title VII Bilingual grant designed to help school districts that had many limited English proficiency (LEP) students. At Edgemere, we recruited teachers who were willing to participate in the program. There were seven teachers that were interested in working with LEP students combined with English speaking students. Each teacher had one bilingual teacher assistant. I went to their classrooms to do demonstrations and help if needed. The program went very well and got strong support from both parents and the community.

The program went so well that, in 1983, I was offered a job as National Origin Coordinator from the Oklahoma State Department of Education which I gladly accepted. I loved my students and teachers at Edgemere, but I also realized that working at the state level would allow me to help LEP students statewide. There was also a financial reality. I needed more money to pay bribes to the Vietnamese government so that my family could come to the United States.

In 1990, my career took a new direction. That year, HB 1017 passed the Oklahoma Legislature, allocating large sums of money for education reform. Part of that package was a new entity, a Minority Teacher Recruitment Center under the State Board of Regents. The law tasked the board with developing a Multicultural Education Program for Oklahoma schools and actively recruiting minorities to consider a career in education. They selected me to head up the initiative as its first director.

The first year everything went well. We set goals. We met those goals. Fifteen school districts were on board, and I was excited about how things were developing. Suddenly, though, the honeymoon was over. I began having difficulties with two staff members, the Teacher/Cadet Coordinator, Dr. J., and my secretary. Dr. J. scheduled meetings and conferences behind my back, often put our primary objective, recruiting minorities into teaching, on the back burner.

After much wrangling, the legislature decided to remove the center from the Board of Regents and place it under the State Department of Education. This pleased me. Before taking this position, I had worked for the State Department and felt the move would benefit everyone. I was elated when the State Superintendent contacted me to see if I was interested in remaining as director of the program. Of course, I was. State hiring laws required that I reapply for the position, but she assured me that was only a formality.

I didn't get the job.

I felt so betrayed. The superintendent had assured me that it was a "done deal." I never saw this coming. At first, I felt lost. For the first time in years, I found myself, master's degree in hand, unemployed. Fortunately, Shady and I had part-ownership of a Chinese restaurant in Oklahoma City. He worked there, so I joined him. The job kept me busy while I struggled with my situation and where to go from here.

Again, as one door closed, God opened another one. I had long realized that "degrees talked" when dealing with people in decision-making positions. It seemed that the more degrees one had, the better people in America felt toward you. The ability behind the degree meant nothing if you didn't have the piece of paper.

I enrolled at the Oklahoma State University and pursued a doctorate in education. In my experience, the degree was often the only way a person in authority could get past physical appearances, so I aimed for the highest level I could. The pieces of paper didn't change who I was, but they did allow others to see past the physically small Asian woman I was. My personal education was the best way to fight the bigotry of the establishment around me.

When all was said and done, I found myself in my last education position. My career ended as head of bilingual education for the Oklahoma State Department of Education. I loved the job and the people and served there until retirement.

Chapter 18

"Surely our griefs He Himself bore,
And our sorrows He carried;
Yet we ourselves esteemed Him stricken,
Smitten of God, and afflicted."

(Isaiah 53:4)

During the four years of struggle getting my family here from Vietnam, other trials occurred closer to home. My husband, Shady, developed hardening of the arteries, requiring five bypasses, leaving him practically an invalid. He could no longer work, so he applied for Social Security disability and was approved. Unfortunately, almost six months passed before he received any money from them. This meant that my state salary had to support us until the payments from the government started.

My family arrived in Oklahoma City during those six months, just before Thanksgiving. With no place else to go and Shady and I barely able to feed ourselves, the six of them had to stay with us. The money we had been sending to Vietnam in bribes was now needed for winter clothes and food.

Luckily, Phan came to our rescue. She and David gave us $10,000 to add a room to the house, buy the family some winter clothing, and help with food. Without that assistance and other help further down the road, I don't know how we would have made it through the winter, let alone the next ten years.

Despite everything, seeing my family safe made the efforts all worthwhile. I assisted them in getting jobs and enrolling the children. Having He already here with a driver's license was a godsend.

Otherwise, Shady would have had to do all the shuttling by himself. Through it all, I knew we would be okay. By any possible means, I would make certain that they succeeded in their new land.

Lan, my adopted daughter and the youngest, proved to have the most difficulty adapting to her new environment. She had been very young when the Communists had taken over South Vietnam and was only fourteen when the family immigrated. She had spent almost her entire life exposed to their propaganda.

In school, Lan had to sit and listen every day to how her grandfather was an evil man – her grandfather who always brought her something from the market as a treat. She could not reconcile the evil her teachers professed with the man she knew and loved.

In mathematics, she learned how weak the American military had been and how many of their planes the "victorious forces" had shot down. She was ridiculed for her mother and her aunt marrying "the enemy."

Coming to America wasn't easy for Lan. She was at an age where friends were important, and she had left all of hers behind. She now lived in the land of the "enemy" her teachers had vilified. Back in Vietnam, life had been hard – much harder than here, but she had known the system and how to work it.

Here, in America, everything was strange.

Then there was Shady, my husband. She hardly knew him and living with us was very difficult. Calling him 'Father' was especially hard at first. She only knew what her Vietnamese teachers had said. He would mistreat her, and part of her just waited for that to happen.

To her surprise, Shady and I showered her with love. We made certain that she had new clothes and plenty to eat. In particular, she had a fondness for donuts. The school was clean and the teachers so patient, especially her English as a Second Language (ESL) teacher, Mrs. Webster who not only taught her but her uncle as well. She was also a close friend of mine. After about six months, Lan, now called Helena, loved her new country. Her only regret was that her friends back in Vietnam couldn't come here as well.

Parts of my family stayed with Shady and me for almost ten years. The children graduated from school, met their loves, and moved out one by one. Hanh, who had taken the English name Tracy, became a computer programmer, while Vinh, Helena, and He all became engineers.

My father, unfortunately, didn't have much time to enjoy his new country before passing on six months after his arrival – a victim of liver cancer. I remember that he got very sick on a Monday and then died on Thursday.

He had told me that his prayer had been to see Phan and I once more. He said that he was very proud of us and hoped that our sisters and brother could learn from our example. He said that his faith had carried him through many trials, and he prayed that we would stay strong in our faith as well. After dad died, with only my stepmother still in my care, I received a plea for help that I could not ignore.

My sister, Vinh, asked if we would like to come to Tucson. She had founded her own company, VAWD, an engineering firm. Her forte had been in math and science, not business. She begged me to come and help with the company's day-to-day operations. She said that the climate in Tucson was wonderful and would be good for Shady as well. How could I say no? I realized that it was time to retire.

At the time of my retirement, I was the Director of Bi-Lingual Education for the State of Oklahoma. I loved my job, but I loved my husband more. I wanted to spend more time with him without the distractions of my career. Somehow, living in the desert area around Tucson for a couple of years sounded great. With his disability and my teacher's retirement, we found that we could more than make ends meet.

When we first moved to Arizona, the idea was

that it would only be temporary. It made sense that we stayed with Vinh and her husband during that time. After all, she had stayed with us for years, and this would only be for a few months.

Unfortunately, my sister had changed a lot since taking on her new role as CEO. She had developed her way of doing things, and her way was not necessarily my way. We constantly disagreed, not only at work but at home as well.

Every morning, Vinh and I would get up early and walk around the neighborhood. During our walks, she would list the things she wanted done that day. The list of my responsibilities grew from day to day.

Before too long, I found that I was busier in retirement than I had been in my full-time job. Shady loved the doctors here and was showing some improvement in his health. Besides, we both were beginning to like the Tucson area. We needed to find a place of our own.

Another downside of living with Vinh was my stepmother. She had moved in with my sister some time before and was not happy with the current housing arrangement. Not only was the proximity with my sister starting to get on my nerves, but my stepmother was also driving Shady crazy. With me gone all day, she had been following him around from place to place, criticizing his every move. When

Vinh and I returned home at the end of the day, she would do nothing but complain about Shady. Vinh informed her that what Shady did was none of her business. I silently applauded.

The biggest obstacle to getting a new house in Tucson was getting a buyer for our home in Oklahoma. When we first decided to move, we listed the home in Del City, hoping for a quick sale. Now, several months later, we were getting concerned that it might not sell at all.

I went to bed that night and prayed that God would help us and send a person who would buy our home. The answer took a couple of additional months, but it came – someone wanted the house. Of course, we had to return to Oklahoma to make some repairs that the buyer required before taking possession—easily done. Once we closed on the home, we were ready to buy – well, almost ready anyway.

Shady and I had once thought homes in Oklahoma were expensive. Tucson prices were exorbitant in comparison. Nothing back in Oklahoma prepared us for the reality of the real estate market here. After a lot of searching, we eventually found our new home nestled in a subdivision on the edge of town. The home was about the size of our previous house, selling for twice the price we had received for our old place, but it was perfect. It sat on almost an acre of land and was right next to the mountains east of Tucson.

Shady's health was still not great. He tired quickly and needed to rest. The surrounding land and the nearby mountains were quite relaxing and were two things he loved about the new place. We realized that this was where we needed to be. We stretched a little and bought it.

The house was perfect for us. Shady loved working in the yard and just sitting in the "Arizona Room" just outside the kitchen, smoking his cigar, and gazing at the mountains. Sometimes, he sat there, lost in his thoughts, for hours on end.

Moving proved to be good for Vinh and me as well. Our working relationship became more relaxed now that Shady and I were no longer living with her family. Shady's sister, Bobbie, and her husband, Kent, would come from Alabama as often as possible. Shady and Kent would play golf while Bobbie and I swapped stories at the house. Life was good. In my mind, this was what retirement was supposed to be.

Figure 2-1
The Wilsons
Nathan, Beeler, Bobbie, and Van

Figure 2-2
Van with English Language teacher (Ms. Susan)

Figure 2-3
My "first" birthday party

Figure 2-4
Van at wedding shower

Figure 2-5
Van and Gloria at wedding shower

Figure 2-6
Wedding shower in Bakersfield

Figure 2-7
Wedding picture, October 1973

Figure 2-8
Shady and Van at wedding in Phoenix, October 1973

Figure 2-9
Shady and Van at wedding in Phoenix, October 1973

Figure 2-10
Phan, Shady, and Van

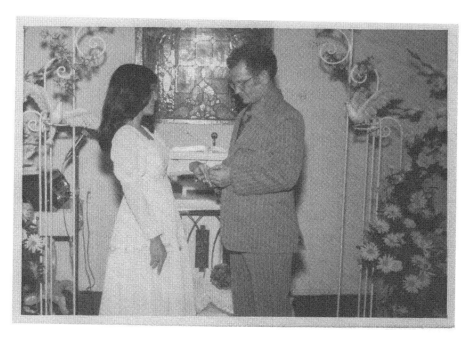

Figure 2-11
Wedding in Phoenix, October 1973

Figure 2-12
Mrs. Andersons Fifth Grade Class at Polk Elementary

Figure 2-13
Van receiving her bachelor's degree

Figure 2-14
Van with co-workers at State Department of Education

Figure 2-15
Summer Refugee Program

Figure 2-16
Van with State Superintendent Sandy Garrett at Van's retirement

Director for minority teacher center named

Thanh Van Anderson

Oklahoma State Regents for Higher Education have named Thanh Van Anderson director of the Minority Teacher Recruitment Center. The center will be operated by the State Regents under a contract with the State Department of Education.

Anderson will serve as the liaison between the State Regents and the State Department of Education in recruiting, placing and retaining minority teachers in Oklahoma public schools.

Formerly the national origin desegregation coordinator for the State Department of Education, Anderson served as adjunct instructor at Langston University and bilingual consultant and fifth grade classroom teacher in the Oklahoma City Public Schools.

In 1987, Anderson was appointed by then Secretary of Education William Bennett to the National Advisory and Coordinating Council on Bilingual Education. A member of the Board of Directors of Oklahoma Women in Education Administration, she also served as vice chair of the Oklahoma Teachers of English to Speakers of Other Languages.

Anderson earned her bachelor's degree in elementary education, a master of education in elementary education and a master of education in school administration from Central State University. She is currently pursuing her Ed.D. at Oklahoma State University.

"Ms. Anderson will play a vital role in helping ensure that the teachers in Oklahoma public schools reflect the ethnic and cultural diversity of our state," said Chancellor Hans Brisch.

"The Minority Teacher Recruitment Center provides an excellent opportunity to enhance the cooperation between higher education and elementary and secondary schools," said Regents' Chairman George B. Kaiser.

Figure 2-6

Article documenting Mrs. Anderson's appointment as the first director of the Minority Teacher Recruitment Center.

報　　　　　　　　　　　亞美視窗

2002 Recipient of Award for Excellence Outstanding Asian-American

Thanh Van Anderson, Ed.D.

Director of Bilingual Education P{rograms
Oklahoma State Department of Education

Dr. Thanh Van Anderson received a Bachelor of Science degree in Elementary Education with a minor in Mathematics and Social Studies in 1978, a Master of Education degree in 1983, and an Elementary Education Administration degree in 1986 from the University of Central Oklahoma. She received a Doctorate of Education degree from the Oklahoma State University in 1997.

Dr. Anderson is currently Director of the Bilingual Education/Title III English Language Instruction and Refugee Children School Impact programs at the Oklahoma State Department of Education. She speaks Vietnamese and English, and has also studied French and Spanish. Dr. Anderson is a bilingual and bicultural educator with twenty-four years of experience in the fields of Bilingual Education, National Origin, and Multicultural Education. Dr. Anderson's work experience includes classroom and university instruction, state and national training in English as a second language (ESL) and language acquisition, director of the Minority Teacher Recruitment Center, administrator of the Human Relations Program, and coordinator for the National Origin Program at the State Department of Education. She assisted in planning and implementing these programs to help minority, limited-English-speaking, and bilingual students mainstream into American school systems.

Dr. Anderson has served on many educational boards and committees, for example, working with the Oklahoma Advisory Council on Bilingual Education; the Oklahoma Association for Bilingual Education, where she is currently president; and was appointed to the National Advisory and Coordinating Council on Bilingual Education by former United States Secretary of Education, Mr. William Bennett, in 1987. She also serves on a dual language advisory board for Oklahoma City Public Schools, and is co-director for Project Four Star, which allows teachers to complete a Master's Degree in Education with an emphasis in English as a second language (ESL) or bilingual education.

Dr. Anderson has made many contributions to education, including organizing the *Dare to Dream Conference* featuring Jaime Escalante, who was the 1990 United States Teacher of the Year and whose portrait was featured in the movie *Stand and Deliver*. In 1995, Dr. Anderson assisted Oklahoma City and Tulsa Public Schools in implementing *Equity 2000*, a program that requires all students to take pre-algebra in eighth grade and geometry in tenth grade to prepare them for college. This program was developed based on research conducted on minority students that showed the narrowing gap in the number of college students dropping out between the minority students and others, and between males and females.

Figure 2-7
Announcement recognizing Mrs. Van Anderson as recipient of the Award for Excellence Outstanding Asian American Award in 2002

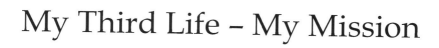

My Third Life – My Mission

Chapter 19

"A joyful heart is good medicine,
But a broken spirit dries up the bones."

(Proverbs 17:22)

Our idyllic life came to a crashing end in 2007, when doctors discovered an eight-centimeter tumor on my liver. Before then, I didn't even have a primary care doctor in Tucson – I never thought I required one. Had I not needed to get my thyroid medication refilled, I might not have had to find a doctor then.

Fortunately, my new doctor and I found each other, and, after my exam, he recommended, as a precaution, that I see a specialist. The history of liver cancer in my family and my ongoing battle with hepatitis-C concerned her.

My doctor referred me to a thyroid specialist, who requested a liver ultrasound. This doctor told me that Asians often had problems with their livers, and it wouldn't hurt to check, especially considering my medical history.

I didn't understand. I felt fine. I wasn't concerned about my liver and didn't feel the treatment was necessary, but when my insurance agreed to pay for the test, I figured why not? I will never forget that day, December 13, 2007. After the test, I went home and went about my everyday life. When the phone rang that afternoon, I was shocked with disbelief when I heard from the doctor. The ultrasound report was back. I had liver cancer.

I was stunned. I don't even remember hanging up the phone. The news shocked me so badly that I broke down and cried, allowing my now limp body to slide to the floor. Shady heard my cries from the other room and ran to me, falling to the floor and embracing me in his arms as I sobbed into his shoulder.

Between my cries, I explained what the doctor had said. I didn't know much about cancer, but I did understand that I had the same type of cancer that had killed my father only a few years earlier. Even though I hated putting this burden on Shady with his health issues, I needed him here with me. I needed his strength to support me now that my own had failed. Quietly, he calmed me down and reminded me of something I already knew. We were partners. We would face this challenge together.

The next day, my doctor put me in touch with a surgeon, who then scheduled a biopsy. Everything was happening too fast. What was the rush? I felt fine, no different than I did before the test. Was it necessary to rush headlong into surgery? It seemed impossible that death grew inside me, ready to snatch me from my life here with Shady. I felt lost and alone even with people around me. I didn't understand what was happening to me, and the explanations I received didn't explain anything about how I was feeling. They were all about technical aspects of the disease – I needed something more.

My fear of my disease only got worse when an intense pain in my abdomen awakened me during the night. Was this my cancer? Had the tumor burst? The only thing I knew for sure was that the pain was intense, so intense that I thought I was dying right now. Truthfully, if the pain didn't lessen soon, I hoped I was dying. Shady called the surgeon I had talked to earlier in the day. Even though it was late at night, someone from his practice answered the phone. The response was simple and short. Shady was to get me to the hospital right away.

I know that I screamed all the way to the hospital with Shady driving the car as fast as he could. Even while the emergency room doctor examined me, I screamed. I was praying – begging for God to take my life – loudly. The doctor finally stopped what she was doing and confronted me, "Please don't pray for God to take you while I am trying to save you!"

The doctor's comment distracted me enough that I managed to get a hold of myself and stifled my screams. I glanced over at my husband, looking so distraught, so pale, so lost, as he stood beside my bed. At that moment, I realized that I was being selfish. I needed to live because he needed me to live.

When the test results returned, the good news was that I wasn't dying – at least not yet. I had gall stones that were causing my pain. The fact that they had appeared at the same time as the cancer was purely chance. The emergency doctor consulted with my surgeon, and they decided that it would be best to "fish out" the stones while he performed the biopsy on the tumor.

The ER doctor gave me some pills to control the pain and allowed me to go home when the pain subsided. The pain's absence left a hole that joy filled. I don't remember ever feeling so relieved. I had to wonder, though. Even though I loved fishing, how do you fish for stones inside the body?

My cancer became Shady's and my secret. At first, I didn't want anyone else to know about my condition. I thought of it as a personal problem, a cross I alone had to bear, and I didn't want to disturb anyone else's lives with my problems. After all, Vinh had her fledgling business. Why would I want to add to her burden?

When Phan visited for a couple of weeks, I changed my mind and unloaded all my problems on her. Though I hated doing so, I needed to do it. Besides, Phan and I loved each other so much. We had been through so many problems and faced so many obstacles throughout our lives that it just seemed right that she should know.

Still, I couldn't believe the relief I felt after telling her. It was incredible. Sharing my burden made it so much easier to bear. Afterward, I realized that I hadn't shared my fears and concerns with God either. When I did so in prayer, peace finally came to my heart. What had I been afraid of?

The "fishing" expedition was successful, as was the biopsy, although the results of the latter were not what I had hoped. The tumor turned out to be cancerous, which turned a beautiful May morning into something dark and scary. The surgeon, Dr. N., removed the tumor, a large part of my liver, as well as my gallbladder.

God had so blessed me with this surgeon, considered to be the best liver specialist in Tucson at that time. He was a caring doctor as well. After I was cured, he told me, "Due to the location of your liver tumor, 60% of your liver had to be removed. To make things riskier, you also had cirrhosis from your hepatitis. With the help of God, your remaining liver recovered."

By this time, I had told my entire family about my condition, and I rejoiced as they rallied around me in support, taking turns staying with me and helping take care of Shady too. After my release from the hospital, they continued to stand by me as I began the ordeals of chemotherapy. Finally, as my life settled into its new routine, they began to relax as well. They went back to their lives and their homes. Some sense of normalcy returned. That lasted until December 2008, when my world once again collapsed.

Chapter 20

"Then the dust will return to the earth as it was, and the spirit will return to God who gave it."

(Ecclesiastes 12:7)

I have heard that God never gives us more than we can handle. I tested that idea one night. The hour was late when I heard Shady calling me from the other side of the bed. We had just enjoyed an excellent evening at Vinh's house. Helena, and her family were visiting, and we had a wonderful time eating and catching up on family news. After returning home, Shady and I prayed together and went to sleep. Everything was normal – until 3 A.M.

Shady's groans awakened me with a start. I was worried. He never did anything like this. He told me it was nothing and that I should go back to sleep, but the moans and groans continued, even louder than before. I asked him if I needed to take him to the hospital, but he declined. He was positive that he was only suffering from indigestion and would be fine in the morning.

At five, he woke me again as he tried to make his way to the bathroom. He was so unsteady that he was hardly able to stand. I wanted to help him but found his weight more than I could handle on my own. I called Vinh's husband, Robert, to come and help. He took only minutes to drive to our place. Once there, he took one look at Shady and called an ambulance.

Things were tense at the hospital. Multiple tests showed that Shady had suffered a mild stroke. Though it might sound strange, this encouraged me.

With everything that had happened in the past year, a mild stroke didn't sound so bad. He might even have a full recovery.

With renewed optimism, I reached out to Shady's three children. Alan and his wife arranged to come out right away, as did his daughter, Tammi. I asked Tammi to contact Shady's other daughter, Marlys. Marlys had never fully come to grips with the divorce and Shady's subsequent remarriage to me, even though it had now been over twenty years. I didn't even have her phone number.

I stayed in the room with Shady as often as the hospital would allow. I even made the conscious decision to stop my chemo for the time being against my doctor's advice. My hospital could not have been farther from Shady's. They were on opposite ends of the city. Travel between the two could take an hour or more depending on traffic.

I felt that staying with him was far more important. I couldn't stand the thought of something happening to him while I was on the other side of town or in transit. I would never have forgiven myself had that occurred. I have never once regretted that decision.

Three months later, in March, my husband, my Shady, passed from this life. I still find it impossible to find the words to relate to the emptiness I felt on that day. He had been my reason for living, my soulmate, and he was no longer here. The house we had shared was so quiet – so vacant without him. His chair in the sunroom seemed out of place without his form sitting in it. I was lost. I no longer wanted to live. Let cancer take me. I didn't care. Without Shady, there was no reason to continue.

Shady had insisted that he did not want a funeral. He wanted no sad faces, no dark clothing. He had requested a cremation followed by a 'Celebration of Life' where all his friends and family could gather to swap stories about him, and that was what I did.

The celebration somehow renewed my strength and confidence. I could sense Shady in the room as people told tales, and laughter spontaneously spread like wildfire among us. I realized that passing from this life should be like this – a celebration of the person and how they affected us. For me, the evening gave me what I needed to carry on.

That next week, I went back to my oncologist to check on the status of my disease. The results were anything but what either of us had expected. The blood test showed the cancer tumor marker was normal. There was no sign of any new cancer — I was not in remission; the cancer was simply gone.

I didn't have to see my oncologist but once per year and only see my primary doctor when I got sick or a six-month follow-up. On that day, God spoke to me in a clear resounding voice.

My doctor was astonished. He told me, "I don't know what purpose God has for you, but people with liver cancer like yours, they just die; they don't get cured." None of my other doctors had an idea of what could have happened. Liver cancer was almost always fatal. People didn't just 'get better' on their own.

I realized at that moment that, even though I felt that my life was over, God was not finished with me. I didn't know what he had in store for me in whatever time I had, but I was committed to finding out.

Before I could discover my path, I needed to do something else. I had been living with hepatitis-C for years, as did many of my countrymen from Southeast Asia. Dr. N. ran some new tests which showed that my hep-C levels were far too high to go untreated. He told me that, untreated, my cancer would return. He suggested that I undergo interferon treatments for my condition immediately.

Why should I do this? I knew that this drug wouldn't cure my hepatitis-C. At this time, no such cure existed. The best the treatment would do was lower the levels in my blood and possibly reduce further damage to my liver. Nonetheless, I felt that I had to move ahead with the medication.

Before starting my treatment, I had

appointments with Dr. D. and Dr. C. They both seemed very nice, still I was uncomfortable being poked and prodded by two male doctors. I felt like a guinea pig, and I guess that was what I was. I didn't complain. Both doctors were donating their time. My insurance paid for the medication, but not the doctors. Dr. D. told me that he had never done this treatment on someone less than one-hundred pounds – I weighed eighty-four.

The first treatment made me want to change my mind. No one told me how awful the treatments would be! The effects of chemotherapy had been severe, but these were far worse than chemo had ever been. Every Monday, I had a blood test and an intravenous treatment every Tuesday.

My body was in agony. It felt as if I were on fire, burning from the inside out. My doctor told me that I was experiencing a known side-effect, an allergic reaction to the drug, and the pain would pass. Easy for him to say. The pain was so intense! Coupled with the mental anguish of losing Shady, I wasn't sure if I could handle it.

The sessions were so debilitating that there was no question but that I needed help. Even if I could drive myself to the treatments, my pain-wracked body would not be able to get me home. I was fortunate that my friend, Kathy, volunteered for the task. She was happy to take me to and from my treatments, eliminating the need for cross-town cab fares.

The kindness of Dr. D. helped me to work through the pain. I didn't have many friends at that time, just Kathy and now Dr. D. He was easy to talk to and I often shared with him the things going in my life. After the treatments, Kathy and I would frequently go out to eat. I so enjoyed this time with them and began looking forward to seeing Dr. D. each week and going out to eat with Kathy.

Kathy was so understanding and helpful in getting me in and out of the car and then into the house. I was so grateful. However, after she left, I would go into the house and hold a pillow over my stomach. Then, I would walk back and forth through the house, crying the entire time until the pain subsided. Not knowing what else to do, I offered my pain to God. Once again, he answered me.

After three months, something amazing happened. The Monday blood test showed that all traces of hepatitis-C in my blood had simply disappeared. After six months, I prayed about whether I should continue the treatments. Of course, my doctor thought I should continue for the full year. After many hours of prayer and discussions with my pastor, his wife, and other members of my church family, I decided. I told my doctor that God had cured me, and I needed to stand on my faith. Dr. D.

made me promise to return to treatments if my disease returned, and I agreed. I firmly believed that Jesus took it from my by his stripes on the cross. My faith was well placed. The disease that I had lived with all my life was gone. I realized that this cure was just another way of God telling me that he wasn't done with me yet.

Chapter 21

"In my distress I called upon the LORD,
And cried to my God for help;
He heard my voice out of His temple,
And my cry for help before Him came into His ears."

(Psalm 18:6)

Of course, the question was, *What was I supposed to do now?* I was in my mid-60s, and most of what I imagined as "God's work" was designed for a much younger person than I. Even though my diseases were gone, my body was still weaker from the effects of chemo and interferon. How could I serve God in my frail and weakened condition?

Despite my desire to serve, I could not see how that could happen. I spent a great deal of time dwelling and praying about this, only to discover that God had put the answer right in front of me all the time.

On my weekly trips to the hospital for treatments and tests, people surrounded me who were suffering as I was. I hadn't noticed them. We tended to stay to ourselves. Socializing somehow didn't seem appropriate. Rarely did anyone smile – laughter was not present. Usually, we all kept our eyes down, afraid of being noticed, not wanting to connect with anyone. The overwhelming emotions were fear and shame – shame for what we perceived to be a curse in the form of the disease.

We didn't *think* we were cursed; we *knew* it. We were afraid because others were afraid. We were aware that other people went out of their way to avoid us, running in fear of cancer, something that they didn't understand – couldn't understand. Each of us was afraid of what might happen next. Might we be spared, or would the disease lead to our own personal encounter with mortality, a meeting that would probably be sooner rather than later?

Our shame stemmed from an underlying feeling that we were somehow responsible for what was happening inside our bodies, or worse, that we had somehow angered God, and the disease was his way of punishing us. Here, among these diseased, hurting, and frightened people, I found my way to answer God's call.

When I started chemotherapy treatments in May 2008, I had dozens of side effects, from sores in my mouth to pains in my abdomen. Nothing tasted good, even those foods I loved. Through my bouts of diarrhea and vomiting, I always thought of my struggles as being personal. I had never concerned myself wondering whether other patients faced the same problems that I did. For me, cancer isolated me into my self-contained world, a world of self-loathing and fear.

In my fear, a thousand questions sprang from my mind. All of them needed answers, but no real answers came. The doctors and nurses gave me textbook responses and tried to be sympathetic, but they often fell short for no other reason than they had no personal reference point. They couldn't understand what I was going through because they never had cancer. True, they were a part of my team, and they took good care of me, but there was no way they could know how I felt – how all cancer patients felt.

Without a firm direction and a plan other than my faith that God would lead me, I decided to volunteer in the cancer unit. I wanted to share my personal experiences and struggles with the disease with other patients who might be asking the same questions.

My spiritual journey was even more important than the physical one. An integral part of my experiences was my faith. My encounters with God helped me find peace during my trials with cancer and my husband's death. My Bible became a vital part of my volunteer "toolkit." I never forced my faith on anyone; rather, I shared how that faith changed me – it made me better able to face my new reality.

After two years cancer-free, I was finally allowed to enter the unit as a volunteer. I reported for duty every Monday from 8 A.M. to 3 P.M. without fail. For me, this was the most important job I had ever had. I would meet the patients as they came for their treatments. I offered them a blanket or pillow, tea, or coffee.

More importantly, I offered a friendly face and an experienced ear to listen – to hear their stories, their fears, their hopes. Sometimes we visited about their disease and how the treatments were going, but more often, we talked about family and life in general.

Not all patients were receptive, of course. Some preferred to be isolated, alone in their thoughts and pain. For those people, I would offer a smile, a pat on the shoulder, and assurance that I was there for them if they ever wanted to talk. I would be ready when they were. Some never responded, but others did, and we became quite close.

When I talked to the patients, I would offer suggestions gleaned from my own experiences. First, I encouraged them to own their illness. They needed to be personally involved with the disease and its treatment. Cancer wasn't a cold that would pass untreated in a week or two. I told them not to be passive about their treatment. Ask questions — demand real answers. Be an active participant. Don't just let things happen.

I suggested that they make a list of questions for the medical staff before their appointment so that there was no chance of forgetting something important in the few minutes with the doctor. A log was such a simple thing, yet I remembered a burning question that often went unasked simply because I forgot about it at the time.

I reminded them to keep a log and record how they felt after the chemo treatments – not just immediately but later that night or sometimes a day or two later. By registering what happened to them, they would see how their bodies reacted to the medicines and look for patterns. Those same notes would give their doctor insights, allowing them to adjust the treatment, making it easier to take.

The log should also show which kinds, and what quantities of food they ate and any adverse reaction their body experienced to a given food or drink so that they could avoid it later. I reminded them that just because a certain food had been fine before did not mean that it was now.

Some patients lost themselves in self-pity, always asking themselves "Why Me?" – a question that had no answer and one that I had asked myself. I quietly reminded them that no one knew how or why we received this cancerous curse. No studies pinpointed exactly why one individual got cancer, and another one didn't.

True, some cancers focus on those who drank alcohol or smoked cigarettes, but most users came away from their experiences without getting cancer. Some never did any of these things and got cancer anyway. I was a living example of that. I didn't drink, yet I still contracted liver cancer.

The hardest conversations came with the patients who thought God was punishing them for their sins. "No, definitely not!" I would tell them the story from John 9:1-3 where we are told, "As he went along, he saw a man blind from his birth. His disciples asked him, 'Rabbi, who sinned, this man or his parents, that he was born blind?' Neither this man nor his parents sinned,' said Jesus, 'but this happened so that the works of God might be displayed in him.'"

Even though I recalled many times in my life when I had not been an angel and, sad to say, had done more than a few bad things during my life, I never blamed my disease on a vindictive God. My God was one of forgiveness and love, not a God of petty vengeance.

I would then look the patient in the eyes and tell them that the best thing they could do was keep a positive mind and keep away from negative people. My own experience had shown how people could react to a person with cancer. I advised them to seek out positive people, people who would support them.

I shared experiences with my own family and friends. I told them of the friends who stopped visiting or talking to me. At the time, I was crushed by what I perceived as a personal betrayal. Later, as I worked my way through my feelings, I came to realize that those friends just didn't know what to say, or they were uncomfortable watching me sicken with a disease they couldn't begin to understand.

I continued, "I let the reactions of my friends wear heavily on me. Please don't get upset when it happens to you. We are so different from each other, and, sometimes, when they are dealing with cancer, people react differently. We cannot change other people; we can only change ourselves. Therefore, focus on yourself what makes you feel good. Cancer is a long journey, and you need to be strong."

After our conversation, the patient would often cry, relating their own experiences with rejections from their friends or family. They told me how good it was to know they were not the only ones who had felt this way. A weight was lifted from their and my shoulders when that happened.

If the patient indicated that they were a Christian, I would take our dialog to a different level. I remembered how vital my church community had been for me, and I would politely ask if they were a member of a church. If they were not, I strongly suggested finding one as soon as possible. I would even invite them to go to church with me if they didn't know where to go. I knew from my own experience how healing the Gospel and the prayers of others could be.

I remembered the members of my church community rallying around me in prayer and volunteering to take me to appointments at the hospital. Their support kept my faith alive at some of the most trying points of my treatment – times when I could have easily given up. I knew that same sense of community and belonging would do the same for these people as well.

Throughout my time at the clinic, I never thought of my volunteering as just a service or a charity. I considered it as a mission that God had given me. This service was the reason he had healed me – so that I could be there for others in need. I took that service seriously, especially when I learned that patients were fellow Christians. More than once, for patients who only had a few weeks left, I would bring Bible scriptures to share with them, and we would talk about the Word.

One patient lived in another town about forty miles from ours. After fighting the disease for some time, she had decided to discontinue her treatments. Her doctor had told her that she only had a few months to live and that additional chemo would only give her a little more time. She wanted to enjoy her life in the little time left. She didn't want the side effects of chemo to spoil those precious moments.

Since she couldn't come to me, I grabbed one of my other friends and went to her, bringing egg rolls, stir-fried noodles, and egg-drop soup along with our friendship. We laughed and prayed all afternoon. God blessed us all that day. A few weeks later, she passed from this life. I mourned her passing yet rejoiced that her pain was no more.

Chapter 22

"But you will receive power when the Holy Spirit has come upon you; and you shall be My witnesses both in Jerusalem, and in all Judea and Samaria, and even to the remotest part of the earth"

(Acts1:8)

Visiting with patients was only one part of my mission. I knew all too well that the people who accompanied the afflicted person were equally vital to that person's well-being. The fact that they were here at the clinic showed that they loved the patient and longed to do more for them. I understood that those friends and family needed to know that they were important too.

From my personal experiences, I knew that all family members started this journey with their patients, overwhelmed by what had happened. There were so many changes happening at far too rapid a pace, which could bewilder a person. Cancer had been a surprise for them and the patient, and they found themselves unprepared to deal with the reality cancer presented.

They tried to be sympathetic but often failed to find words because they could not identify with what the patient was experiencing. They couldn't see that the patient often had no idea how they would feel from one minute to the next. How could they?

Human nature screamed that they had to do something – anything. They hated feeling helpless. Most of the time, it never occurred to them that all the patient needed was to talk, have a conversation. Let the patient tell them what they needed – wanted. The best thing one could do was just listen to them.

I would state the most obvious yet most ignored fact in my conversations with the family. "You must accept what has happened." A rolling of their eyes almost always followed my statement. I continued by saying, "Acceptance brings its own level of peace. It allows everyone to relax, just a little, just enough to move forward."

I realized that just the word 'cancer' brought all kinds of images to mind – none of them good. The family needed to resist the denial that the human mind instinctively embraced. The cancer was here. The tumor was not just going to go away. Any other attitude would be a rejection of the facts.

Families would ask me, "How do I remain positive, when my father/mother/sister/brother is lying there hurt and exhausted before me." It would be so easy to think that maybe they would feel better if they fixed the person's favorite food. The problems came when the patient rejected their efforts. The family couldn't realize that chemo changed the patient's tastes and appetite. They may have loved tamales a month ago, but now they only brought disgust and nausea. Often, patients would lash out at a family member trying to help, hurting them deeply because the patient was also frustrated. Unfortunately, sometimes the hurt ran so deep that the family member gave up, left, and never returned.

To those family members, I beg you to forgive.

The slight was not intentional. The patient's attack on you was an expression of frustration and fear, nothing more. It was the cancer talking, not the person. When you leave, you take hope with you. Come back. Try again.

Words for the friends and family of those with cancer

"This is My commandment, that you love one another, just as I have loved you. Greater love has no one than this, that one lay down his life for his friends."

(John 15:12-13)

Your friend or a family member has cancer, but he or she is still the same person you knew before all this happened. They desperately need normality in their lives, and like it or not, their family and friends are the closest thing to normal they have right now. Try your best not to treat them any differently.

Because you are so close to them, it will be far too easy to whip out the laptop and do "research" to "help" them. Please don't fall into this trap. Forcing them to eat things they don't want because some television show or website says it's good for them would be a disaster for both of you. Don't force them to eat at all!

Their body knows when it needs to eat and what sounds good to them at the time. Give it to them. If they want a hamburger and fries, that's what they should have. Pizza? No problem. Trying to "go organic" or cooking only with "healthy" foods may not always be the best way.

Remember, healthy food encourages weight loss, and losing weight is not the best thing for them right now. They need their strength to fight the disease and the chemo. Support your patient – serve your patient, don't try to control them. That will only push them away.

The best way to help your friend or family member is to focus on what you can do. The natural thing would be to blame the disease on something or someone. Sometimes, it is hard to accept that no one was to blame. Cancer is there – period. No one benefits from dwelling on it or pushing it aside.

What to do? Consider several things: enjoy a meal, bring pictures of fun times shared with family and friends, or maybe laugh with them. Swing in the playground if that's what they want. Create a future that includes them no matter how long or short that future might be. Do things that they want to do, even if you hate it. Shady asked me repeatedly to watch him play golf. I refused. I so regret not granting his wish.

Most importantly, you need to try dealing with the patient's fear. This cancer journey is a frightening one. Everything about what they are experiencing is unknown. They must know that they are not fighting the battle alone.

I remember my own family; how important it was that they accepted me unconditionally. I was so frightened. I didn't need advice. I wasn't looking for a surrogate parent telling me what to do and what not to do, what to eat and what not to eat. I needed someone to listen to me as I voiced my fears and concerns without any judgment. My life was full of change. I didn't need any more pressure from those I loved. These patients don't either.

Most importantly, I beg you to avoid discussing the disease unless the patient wants to talk about it, especially talking around the patient while they are within earshot like they are not there. Trust me; they will start the conversation if one is needed.

I always hated when a conversation started, "I had a friend with cancer, and they …" How could I tell my family that there is no comparison between my cancer and their friend's disease? Each of our bodies is different – every cancer is different.

No two journeys are the same, and that's what this is, a journey – not across a street or to a different country – this is a journey through life. In these travels through uncharted lands, no two people react to chemo the same way; some lose their hair, some don't. Some lose their appetite; others eat like a horse. Like no two cancers are alike, no two treatments work the same either.

Whenever someone assumed that they "knew" what to do because they read it online, my frustrations grew to a new level. I knew that they were only trying to help and felt compelled to do anything they could, but their comments didn't help. They only made me feel worse, and from my pain and confusion, I would often lash out at them – the people who loved me more than anyone in my life.

Later, I would offer an apology for the things I said. I realized that they were with me at this time out of an abundance of love for me, and I appreciated that so much more than I could express. I thanked them over and over for how generously they gave themselves to me. I would explain that I meant no offense, how my words were "cancer frustration" speaking aloud. The words flew out of my mouth in my anger and pain. At the time, I had no control. I prayed that my apology was enough to salve the wounds I had created.

I mention this because your person will do the same. They will get frustrated by a lack of progress or by nerves worn thin by the pain of treatment. They won't mean a word of it. Let their comments roll off your back like rain, and, when they finish, hug them – hard.

Finally, please ask your patient about their faith. Now is the time when they need to come to grips with what they believe. For me, that involved reading and teaching the Bible. For your patient, their need may be different. Do they want to go to church? If so, move heaven and earth to ensure they can get

226

there. Take them, regardless of your personal feelings, beliefs, or schedule. Stand beside them as they search for answers from God. Right now, they are the important one, not you.

In my experience, I found that these observations on what patients and their families were going through were effective. Often, people opened-up to me when they wouldn't talk with anyone else. Throughout their treatment, I could see them becoming more comfortable when talking with their family and their family with them. It was beautiful.

There was one lady who would come from Phoenix to visit her sick father every week. Every week, she made a point of taking him to get a Wendy's chocolate frosty, his favorite treat. It is not the cost of the gift; it is the time spent that is important.

A young couple changed their wedding plans so that they could be certain their afflicted parent could attend. That took a great deal of effort, but the memories will last forever.

During these talks, a great weight appeared to lift from their shoulders. For that easing, I thanked God for allowing our paths to cross. There would be one less thing to worry about that day.

Sadly, not every patient survived their journey. The hatred of God could run deep in these people and in their family members. I considered helping these people face the hereafter to be my greatest challenge – a challenge only made greater when the patient was young, or worse, a child.

They could not envision a loving God who would allow someone so young to suffer so much and then take them. Over and over, I would remind them that the disease was not of God. Whatever had caused this to afflict them was not retribution for unknown sins. I reminded them that God – my God – would be the one waiting for them, ready to take their pain and suffering away as he welcomed them into his kingdom.

Every time patients stopped blaming themselves for their disease was a blessing. Every smile was a joy. Every husband who hugged their wife without fear of hurting them was a godsend. Every person whose faith sprung anew because of something I said or something I did was a gift that was beyond price. I lived for these moments – my mission.

God did not call me to be a prophet or a healer. My degree wasn't in social work, psychology, or theology. No one would ever consider me an expert in these areas. However, God knew what he wanted. God called me to be a witness, a witness of the things that happened to me – the illnesses that attacked my body and the God that healed me.

I am still not a great speaker. As a Vietnamese

immigrant, my English was fair at best. I depended on my Lord to speak through me, to help me find the right words to help others on their journey. I can't think of a single time that he let me down.

Right now, I am on my third journey, and I am afraid that this one will be my last. I accept that. My doctor asked if I would be interested in a new drug trial. I heartily agreed, not to lengthen my life but to add to the vault of knowledge so that someday a cure can spare another life from the trials of cancer. That is how I feel it should be. In the end, I will live, or I will die. Either way is fine by me.

I often look back on my life and the people who have counted me as family or friends. So many people are no longer here. My mother died when I was three, along with my unnamed brother. My father succumbed to liver cancer only a short time after surviving the Viet Cong Reeducation Camps. The Wilsons...my Shady. So many lives have intertwined with mine through the grace of God, and I find myself incredibly blessed that they did.

As I said in the beginning, death and I are old friends. I don't fear him. When he does come for me in the fullness of time, I will gladly take his hand and let him lead me home where Shady and my Lord patiently wait for me.

One last thing…

By Thanh Van Anderson, December 2021

After a wonderful family reunion in Hawaii, I am back in Tucson. I planned the trip because I am the one who brings our family together, and I wanted all of us together one last time. I realized that my time was short, and I wanted to make the most of what time I had left.

The trip went very well; everyone enjoyed our time together. I greatly appreciated my sister Phan and her husband, Will, for hosting the family reunion in their beautiful house on Hilo. While I'm at it, I must brag about my family members a little. They love me so much and did so much for me.

Phan cooked my two favorite meals: lamb chops and grilled shrimp. I had tried to imitate the recipe at home, but no matter how often I watched her cook them, mine never turned out the way hers did. They melted in your mouth! While we were on Kona, she also took our entire family to my favorite restaurant. The trip was only made better because my surgeon Dr Taylor Rail and her husband were able to join us.

Robert and Vinh rented a house in a gated community on Kona with four bedrooms. We stayed there for five days and four nights sharing stories and eating food. As a treat, Robert cooked delicious salmon and steaks for us to enjoy. Robert and Vinh's daughter, Chelsea, was so sweet. She always sat next to me and made certain that I always had enough water.

My brother He and his wife, Anna along with their children Harold and Taylor brought in tons of food from Oklahoma including some Oklahoma fish that He had caught. We had it for dinner on Christmas evening. Anna also cooked our favorite Pho. Pho just doesn't taste that good in Tucson. Harold became our breakfast specialist. He really knew how to cook bacon. Taylor was so sweet. She made sure I had everything I needed and would sit by me while we watched television.

Tracy and I don't cook as well as the others, so we took over clean-up. Helena and Taylor set up the table. Everybody worked together and enjoyed each other's closeness.

That Christmas evening, we sat around and sang Christmas carols. I reflected on how, despite our differences, we love each other and will always be there for each other.

The family did me a great service while we were together. One night, they shared their thoughts about me and how I had affected them. It was wonderful to see how our experiences together had helped them to grow. My heart was touched. Things had affected my family that I didn't even remember. I felt embraced by their love. My message to you, my friends, is to not wait until the funeral. Tell your loved ones how you feel about them – right now.

Barring God's intervention, I will soon be gone from this world, and I am fine with that. I feel so blessed that God has allowed me to see how I affected my family over the years. Each of them: Phan and Will, He and Anna, Vinh and Robert, Tracy, and Helena and Linh, along with all their children shared their thoughts on our time together – how I had managed to affect the outcome of their lives. They all changed and, in turn, changed me.

This cancer reminds us that time on earth is short and very valuable. None of us knows what will happen tomorrow. There are thousands of ways to die. Mine just has a name – cancer. All we can do is enjoy the moments we have and be kind to one another.

Before we left Hawaii, I asked my family to continue to get together at least once each year, even in my absence. I want them to build good memories for themselves and their children after I die.

I am sharing this with you because I would like to leave one final word. "For to me, to live is Christ, and to die is gain." St. Paul wrote this to the Philippians almost two thousand years ago, and the words still ring true for us today. I want to use his words to inspire other Christian patients to follow me and turn their last stage of life into a witness for Christ to the world. We should be bravely living until we see Christ face to face.

Van

Figure 3-1

High School Reunion 2016

Figure 3-2

High School Reunion 2016

Figure 3-3
Van, Luyen, and niece, Nga

Figure 3-4
Van and niece, Nga

The Four Faces of Chemotherapy

Figure 3-4
Before starting chemo

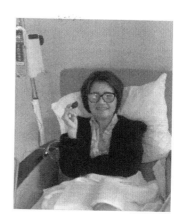

Figure 3-5
First Chemo Treatment

Figure 3-6
Hair gone – Do rag on

Figure 3-7
Wigs work

Figure 3-8
Family at Black Sand Beach in Hawaii, 2021

Back row Ryan, He, Van, Anna, Harold
Front row Helena, Tracy, Vinh, and Taylor

Figure 3-9
Family portrait in traditional attire (taken before Shady died)
Front row: Chelsea (Vinh and Robert's daughter), Taylor, and Harold (He and Anna's children)
Second row: Helena (my daughter), Tracy (Hanh), Vinh, Hoang thi Noi (stepmother), Van, He, Anna
Third row: Khoa (Tracy's son), Truman (Vinh's son), Robert (Vinh's husband), Shady

Figure 3-10
Taylor, Harold (both are children of He and Anna) Ryan (my grandson, Helena and Linh's son)
Chelsea (Vinh and Robert's daughter)

Figure 3-11
Van and Dr. Riall, Van's surgeon

Figure 3-12
Front row: Dr. Martine (Van's friend), Van, Dr. Joe Gerber (Cancer survivor), Suzan (Joe's wife)
Back row: Singer and waitress from restaurant

Figure 3-13
Barbara, Van, Pamala (Husband, Steve died of cancer)

Figure 3-14
Bench dedication for Shady at McDonald Park, Tucson

Figure 3-15
One of Van's Bible Study groups

Figure 3-16
Van's home Bible Study group

Testimonies

"And when I came to you, brethren, I did not come with superiority of speech or of wisdom, proclaiming to you the testimony of God."

(1 Corinthians 2:1)

Melva Garzelloni wrote this about her son who fell victim to his cancer.

My son Josh was diagnosed with cancer in 2015, and during his chemo treatments we met a volunteer like no other. Her name was Van. We knew right away that she cared. She not only cared about Josh, but she also cared about our whole family. Sometimes I would accompany him, sometimes my daughter or granddaughter would, and we all looked forward to seeing her. Josh made sure that he went for treatment on the days that she was there.

We learned that she was a cancer survivor herself. She understood. She got it. She encouraged us, empathized with us, and made sure that we knew where her hope came from - The Lord Jesus Christ. My son had not been going to church for many years. She invited him to come to her church, and even though he wouldn't go when I asked him, he said, "Sure" to Van. True to his word, he went, and continued to go on Wednesday nights whenever he was able. I went with him and figured out fairly quickly that we weren't the only ones that were there because of Van's invitation and encouragement.

She introduced us to people she met at the cancer center, the gym, etc. It was clear that her main goal was to share the Gospel and to bring others into the Kingdom. She has become a dear friend to me and continues to pray for my family. Out of a heartbreaking experience, I have the best gift a mother can have - to see her son return to the Lord. I know I'll see him again, and I have Van to thank for that.

Frances Carlson suffered from breast cancer. She wrote.

I was diagnosed with a very aggressive Her2 breast cancer in 2015. My PC doctor referred me to a surgeon, Kelly Farve, who convinced me to have a mastectomy rather than a lumpectomy. At the time I was scheduled for eye surgery which was crucial for my continued eyesight. There was a lot going on at once and remembering what my mother went through with both radiation and chemo for her lung cancer, I was skeptical, not sure if I wanted to go through it all.

I went ahead with the eye surgery on September 3rd. I even succumbed to having a port installed. However, I remained unsure about starting chemo. I was scared. It wasn't until November that I decided to move forward with chemo and that's when I met a volunteer, Van Anderson. She will never know how much her kind words, spiritual guidance, and friendship helped me. I watched her minister to others in the treatment room always with a friendly smile. Her encouragement helped so many that it was impossible not to like her.

There were times when we brought food in for all to enjoy. It made the time go by and it was a time, while so many were undergoing treatment, for fellowship, and Van was instrumental in helping all of us work our way through a difficult time.

I cherish her friendship and sadly, I am now aware that her own cancer has returned, and her time may be short. I pray that her suffering will be short lived, and that God will bless her every day with the same loving attention she so readily gives all others. She is a blessing.

Finally, this note was sent from a fellow traveler on the journey, Pamela Torbet.

I met Van in either late September or early October of 2016. My husband, Steve, was on his last leg of his colon cancer battle. On our first visit to Arizona Oncology, we met Van. She was volunteering there to provide hope for so many people as she was past seven years as a liver cancer survivor.

Shortly after we arrived, Van came over to introduce herself and to ask if she could get anything for us – a warm blanket, a snack, or a drink. My husband was reading his Bible, and Van asked us if we were Christians. I told her yes, and she shared that she was a Christian as well. We were immediate friends. We began to look forward to seeing her every Monday.

Van was not the only volunteer, but there was no other like Van. She genuinely loved and cared for each patient that she ministered to. Eventually, my husband was transferred to a different oncologist who practiced at University Hospital, and we lost contact with Van. We had never shared any contact information. Our lives were centered on in and out of hospitals until, on Christmas Eve, 2016, my husband was placed in hospice care where he went home to God on December 28.

A short time later, I determined to try to find Van. It occurred to me that I might find her on Facebook, which I did. I sent her a personal message which she answered right away. We made plans to get together and again became fast friends. She made sure that I got out of the house, and we did things that we both enjoyed – going out to the park, eating at our favorite places, and window shopping.

One day, Van called me to tell me about a patient at the cancer center that she didn't feel had much time to live. She asked me to go with her to Vail to see the lady. Of course, I agreed. Van arranged to pick me up and arrived loaded down with food – roasted chicken, vegie plate, a dozen doughnuts, and so many other things that I can't mention them all. We spent the afternoon talking with her about Jesus and salvation. I remember that she cried. The lady seemed so good that day that Van and I were shocked when she died only two days later. I am so glad that we went when we did.

After Van's diagnosis with pancreatic cancer, she could no longer volunteer at the cancer center. She and I began walking every morning. Many times, we went to McDonald Park where she would always gather a group together to visit. Van had a bench made and placed in the park in honor of her husband, Shady, who loved to go there and sit.

My friendship with Van is hard to put into words. I love her immensely and I often refer to her as my backdoor friend. She is the only friend I have who calls my guest room "her room." Sometimes she will call up and ask if I've eaten. If I answer, "no", then it would not be unusual for her to say "Fine, make some for me too. I'm coming over!" We always enjoy the time we spend together. She is more like family than just a friend.

God definitely knew what he was doing when he knit this friendship together. We both feel comfortable sharing the deepest recesses of our hearts and share secrets that we would never tell anyone else.

About the Author

Dr. Thanh Van Anderson has always been an educator, leader, and source of inspiration. As a child in Vietnam, she guaranteed that her siblings could pursue their education even when it meant her postponing her schooling. After emigrating to the USA, she studied mathematics and in 1997 received a Doctorate in Education from Oklahoma State University.

Both in public schools and at the university level, Van specialized in teaching English As a Second Language, writing, and mathematics. In her fifth-grade class, nearly every student finished both fifth- and sixth-grade mathematics in a single year. The children were Black, White, Asian, Hispanic, and Native Americans.

Van organized the Dare to Dream Conference featuring Jaime Escalante, whose story was featured in the film, *Stand and Deliver*. She then assisted Oklahoma City and Tulsa Public Schools in implementing Equity 2000. This program required all students to take pre-algebra in eighth grade and geometry in tenth grade to prepare them for college better.

Van was instrumental in developing Oklahoma House Bill 1017, which established multicultural education and led to creating the Minority Teacher Recruitment Center, where she served as its first director.

She served on the Governor's Advisory Council on Bilingual Education. She was Director of the Bilingual Education/Title III English Language Instruction and Refugee Children. She became certified by Franklin Covey Company to train Oklahoma educators on The Seven Habits of Highly Effective People, based on a book written by Dr. Stephen R. Covey.

Van was appointed to the National Advisory and Coordination Council on Bilingual Education by former U.S. Secretary of Education William Bennett; to the Associated Catholic Charities Board of Directors by the Archbishop of Oklahoma, Eusebius J. Beltran; and to Governor David Walters' Advisory Council on Asian American Affairs.

Her volunteer work has included service with Vietnamese Community Boat People S.O.S. and Vietnamese, Chinese, Korean, Laotian communities. She helped Hispanic parents and students in rural and urban school districts across Oklahoma.

Among her many awards and recognitions are the 2000 Outstanding Title VII Administrator Award, Asian Society Awards, and 1994 Multicultural Citizen of the year.

Van retired in 2007 and moved to Tucson, Arizona, where she has been a volunteer at the Tucson Cancer Center and facilitator of a women's Bible study with the Eastside Assembly of God. When the church temporarily closed due to COVID-19, Van started to go to MacDonald Park to walk and share her faith.

Even after her second cancer diagnosis, Van continues to live a full and exciting life, very involved with her church and friends. She says, "The cancer might get my body but not my soul." Van wishes for each of her readers to enjoy life and be faithful to God, for He loves you and is always with you. "Let Him Be your sterling wheel to lead your life. He is at the door waiting for you to invite Him in to be a part of your life. All of you, regardless of race, are beautiful in His eyes. You are very special; He has distinguished you from any other person. You are his child, smart, caring, and genuine. Don't let what other people say about you become your reality. Your skin color is not stopping you from being a success in this world. May God bless you with a full life."

About the Writer

Mr. Bruce Baker is a writer of narrative non-fiction as well as biographies. He has published several op-ed pieces and short fiction for literary journals. *Faith Through Trial* is his second biography. His first major work, *The Chance: The true story of one girl's journey to freedom,* received many favorable reviews from critics around the country. A third book, *Green Eyes,* is due to be out at the end of 2022.

In addition to his writing efforts, Mr. Baker is also an accomplished photographer having won several awards in the Oklahoma City area. He is a retired teacher from Oklahoma City where he currently lives with his wife, Deborah.

www.soonershoot.com
soonershoot@gmail.com

Bibliography

"French Rule Ended, Vietnam Divided."
     Encyclopædia Britannica, Encyclopædia
     Britannica, Inc.,
     https://www.britannica.com/event/Vietnam-
     War/French-rule-ended-Vietnam-divided.

VnExpress. "Baked for 100 Years: Clay Houses Stand
     Tall in Northern Vietnam - VnExpress
     International." VnExpress International – Latest
     News, Business, Travel and Analysis from
     Vietnam,
     https://e.vnexpress.net/news/travel-
     life/baked-for-100-years-clay-houses-stand-
     tall-in-northern-vietnam-3461342.html.

Elkind, Jessica. "'The Virgin Mary Is Going South':
     Refugee Resettlement in South Vietnam, 1954–
     1956." *Diplomatic History*, vol. 38, no. 5, Oxford
     University Press, 2014, pp. 987–1016,
     https://www.jstor.org/stable/26376620.

"Vietnam War Timeline." Edited by History.com
     Editors, *History.com*, A&E Television Networks,
     September 13 2017,
     https://www.history.com/topics/vietnam-
     war/vietnam-war-timeline.

Britannica, The Editors of Encyclopaedia. "Ngo Dinh Diem". Encyclopedia Britannica, January 7 2021, https://www.britannica.com/biography/Ngo-Dinh-Diem. Accessed October 27 2021.

Britannica, The Editors of Encyclopaedia. "Viet Cong". Encyclopedia Britannica, February 11 2020, https://www.britannica.com/topic/Viet-Cong. Accessed October 27 2021.

Spector, Ronald H. "Vietnam War". Encyclopedia Britannica, 6 Jul. 2021, https://www.britannica.com/event/Vietnam-War. Accessed 29 October 2021.

Britannica, The Editors of Encyclopaedia. "betel". Encyclopedia Britannica, 30 Aug. 2013, https://www.britannica.com/plant/betel. Accessed 1 November 2021.

Lacey, Cindy Sui and Anna. "Asia's Deadly Secret: The Scourge of the Betel Nut." BBC News, BBC, 22 Mar. 2015, https://www.bbc.com/news/health-31921207.

"Flight from Indochina - UNHCR." UNHCR.org, UNHCR, https://www.unhcr.org/3ebf9bad0.pdf.

Barker, Phan Nguyen. "Walking Through Mist." East
Hawaii Cultural Center, East Hawaii Cultural
Center, Dec. 2020,
https://ehcc.org/sites/default/files/Walking
%20Through%20Mist_%20PNB%20Booklet.pdf

Vandever, Leslie. "What Are the Side Effects of
Hepatitis C Treatment?" Healthline, Healthline
Media, 2 Jan. 2020,
https://www.healthline.com/health/hepatitis-
c/side-
effects?utm_source=google&utm_medium=
cpc&utm_cmpid=1581541350&utm_ad
gid=58180770685&utm_adid=296992978519
&utm_network=g&utm_device=c&am
p;utm_keyword=hep+c+treatment+side+effects
&utm_adpos=&utm_gclid=CjwKCAi
Ah_GNBhAHEiwAjOh3ZOBmG8nKGo7gHSBU
OhcfkSC3Uud5eK6KLF7oJDJ91xPZGIYAt92tTxo
CmH0QAvD_BwE&gclid=CjwKCAiAh_G
NBhAHEiwAjOh3ZOBmG8nKGo7gHSBUOhcfk
SC3Uud5eK6KLF7oJDJ91xPZGIYAt92tTxoCmH
0QAvD_BwE#takeaway.

"Chemotherapy for Liver Cancer." *American Cancer
Society*, https://www.cancer.org/cancer/liver-
cancer/treating/chemotherapy.html.

The Holy Bible: Updated New American Standard
Bible: Containing The Old Testament and the
New Testament. Zondervan Pub. House, 1999.

Made in the USA
Columbia, SC
25 May 2022

60887132R00150